The church in earlier times spoke in depth and at length regarding the virtues and our need to acquire them. In his latest work, *The Virtuous Life*, Bishop Robert Solomon helps break a long drought in the critical explication of the character of God as revealed in Jesus and as intended for the bride of Christ. A leader of the global church, Bishop Solomon brings his maturity and gentleness to fruition in this transforming study on virtue and its display through the nine fruit of the Spirit.

This deeply Christ-centered and thoroughly biblical work offers broad application to worldwide Christianity. Bishop Solomon illustrates every virtue as coming in and through the life and ministry of Christ and then helps readers integrate those same virtues into heart, home, workplace, and world. In that the church needs immense help to swim against cultural currents that drown virtue, this study is, I believe, of critical importance to God's people today. Robert Solomon has given the global church a gift. I will place this text on "the must read" list for my students.

Rev Dr Stephen L Martyn
Associate Professor of Spiritual Formation
Asbury Theological Seminary, USA

Serious works on the fruit of the Spirit are few and far between despite the recent tsunami of books on spirituality. In *The Virtuous Life*, Bishop Solomon has therefore done the church a great service by drawing our attention to these important aspects of the spiritual life. This exposition of the fruit of the Spirit is especially significant because it is grounded in the character and purpose of the triune God, and portrays love as the fountain of the different virtues. Bishop Robert Solomon has once again written a book of uncommon wisdom, insight and elegance. The thoughtful and prayerful reading of this book will surely be a transformative experience.

Dr Roland Chia
Chew Hock Hin Professor of Christian Doctrine
Trinity Theological College, Singapore

Once again Bishop Solomon has discerned the times and perceived the scriptural guidance for our times. Ancient Christians talked about living the virtuous life, by which they meant living by and in the Holy Spirit. Bishop Solomon understands this truth about virtue — that it is, both power and habit, grace and cultivation — and he explains how we can participate in the virtuous life of Christ today. I highly recommend this book not only for Christians serious about their Christian life, but especially for missionaries and for others in leadership.

Rev Dr Scott W Sunquist
Dean and Professor of World Christianity,
Fuller Theological Seminary, USA

In a contemporary church often dominated subtly by the ways of the world, and in a world searching for what it means to be fully human, this is an important book. Bishop Robert Solomon gives a timely reminder of the centrality of Christian character through an accessible and exciting exploration of the fruit of the Spirit, as seen supremely in Jesus.

Rev Professor David Wilkinson
Principal, St John's College, Durham University, UK
Professor, Department of Theology and Religion, Durham University

In *The Virtuous Life*, Bishop Dr Solomon displays his depth of understanding of Scripture as well as his spirituality in life. In clear simple language, he unpacks for the readers the fruit of the Spirit in the context of the Father's eternal purpose, the character of the Son of God and the ministry and power of the Holy Spirit; he helps the reader explore how the fruit of the Spirit can take shape and grow in our daily lives and relationships. I especially appreciate the well-thought-out questions for reflection that he provides at the end of each chapter that can be used for deeper personal reflection or group discussions.

Bishop Terry Kee
President
National Council of Churches of Singapore

There is a crisis in both church and society owing to the devaluing of virtue. People need to be convinced that living a life of virtue is necessary, desirable and possible. Bishop Solomon uses his knowledge of both the world and the Word to present a health-giving antidote to this crisis.

Dr Ajith Fernando
Teaching Director
Youth for Christ, Sri Lanka;
Author, *Deuteronomy: Loving Obedience to a Loving God.*

Bishop Robert Solomon provides a highly accessible and straightforward account of the relationship between godly character and the fruit of the Spirit. Biblical and practical, this book brings together Bishop Solomon's insights as a scholar/pastor and trained physician to show how faith, doctrine and spiritual well-being are inextricably woven together. This volume is valuable both for individual and group study and the questions for reflection at the end of each chapter provide practical guidance to understand and thus nurture Christian virtue.

Rev Dr Thomas Harvey
Academic Dean
Oxford Centre for Mission Studies, UK

Like the good doctor he is, Dr Solomon has written a good book. Virtue is viewed as the healing of the entire person so that one can be saved to be sanctified for the glory of God. Virtue is but the fruit of the Spirit, the subtitle of the book being "Cultivating the fruit of the Spirit". This fruit (singular) is ninefold yet one, rich despite what appears to be a grammatical mistake. Dr Solomon wisely points out that God the Spirit does not act alone, but acts together with God the Father and God the Son in Trinitarian theology, in growing the virtuous life in any Christian. Hence the eight virtues of joy, peace, patience, kindness, goodness, faithfulness, gentleness and self-control are but expressions of the ninth, love, which because it is paramount, it is put first in Galatians 5:22. Each of these nine virtues has a chapter explaining them. I commend a careful reading of this book to the Christian who wants to grow in the grace and truth of our Lord Jesus Christ. Dr Solomon once again demonstrates his love for God's Word in the abundant references he makes to God's Word as well as the writings of many virtuous Christians.

Dr Lee Soo Ann
President
Bible Society of Singapore

THE VIRTUOUS LIFE

Cultivating the Fruit of the Spirit

ROBERT M SOLOMON

Published by Genesis Books
An imprint of ARMOUR Publishing Pte Ltd
Kent Ridge Post Office
P.O. Box 1193
Singapore 911107
Email: sales@armourpublishing.com
enquiries@armourpublishing.com
Website: www.armourpublishing.com

21 20 19 18 17 16 15 14 13 12
10 9 8 7 6 5 4 3

Cover design by Sharlyn Solomon

Printed in Singapore

ISBN 13 : 978-981-4305-95-2
ISBN 10 : 981-4305-95-2

National Library Board, Singapore Cataloguing-in-Publication Data

Solomon, Robert M., 1956-
The virtuous life : cultivating the fruit of the spirit / Robert M Solomon. – Singapore : Genesis Books, 2012.
p. cm.
Includes bibliographical references and index.
ISBN : 978-981-4305-95-2 (pbk.)

1. Spiritual life - Christianity. I. Title.

BV4501.3
248.4 -- dc23 OCN794708442

CONTENTS

PREFACE

To the glory of the Triune God
Who is at work for, in, and among us
to save us
and make our lives fruitful.

In today's secular world, the old connection between character and competence is being gradually eroded. Leaders were at one time invariably expected to be virtuous persons. Now, however, they are invariably expected to be competent. Their private lives and whether they live virtuously or not is increasingly seen as irrelevant so long as they can deliver in their jobs.

The crack in popular attitudes between character and competence has widened and extended itself into the church. Edward Farley, in his survey of the nature of theological education in the past 200 to 300 years describes the primary paradigms of three successive periods.[1] During the first period, theological education was understood primarily as training in piety. The focus in the second period was on scholarship and the development of academic disciplines in the seminary. The final period contains the paradigm of theological education as professional training.

The emphasis has changed over time from spirituality to scholarship to practical skills. The great concern is the disconnection between the three — that is, the church may be increasingly looking for the skilled leader without due regard to his spirituality and scholarship. Anyone who has entrepreneurial skills can rise rapidly in the many social ladders in church.

What may be true for the pulpit would also be true for the pews. We are seeing a church culture of activism (much of it increasingly is spiritually mindless), a focus on "how to" spiritual techniques, an appetite for instant solutions and a flexing of organisational muscle. In this environment, true spiritual formation in Christ tends to get neglected or ignored. Restlessness is replacing reflection.

Short attention spans and increasing boredom result in the loss of attention to the Word and the sustained and disciplined cultivation of Christian character and the virtuous life in Christ.

I cannot agree more with theologian Philip Kenneson's astute observations about the contemporary church:

> "(I)t is quite possible for the church to be both growing and yet not bearing the fruit of the Spirit. What is happening in many cases is that the church is simply cultivating at the center of its life the seeds that the dominant culture has sown in its midst. As a result, the seeds that the Spirit has sown are all but being choked out, and the fruit that is being brought to harvest has little or no likeness to the Spirit's fruit."[2]

It is in this context that this book about the fruit of the Spirit is written. Paul wrote to the Galatian church which faced the danger of becoming derailed from the journey in which they had started well. This Pauline epistle was in fact the earliest New Testament document to be written. It was a time when the Christian church was in its infancy and its identity was being formed. Was it a Jewish sect or a new society created around Christ by the Holy Spirit?

The Galatian church seemed to be having serious problems in this area. Thanks to false itinerant teachers who were teaching "another gospel," a legalism was setting in which threatened the spiritual life of the church. The Galatian Christians faced the danger of becoming adept at playing religion without paying attention to the transforming grace of God and the inner changes that must take place when such grace touched their lives. They were in danger of mistaking their religious actions for the change in character that must take place in their lives — rejecting the gospel of grace for a false spirituality of manufactured piety.

Paul dealt with the issue by contrasting the true gospel and its counterfeit, faith and works, liberty and legalism, servants and sons, and the Spirit and the flesh. He warned the Galatian Christians that they needed to know how to differentiate the works of the flesh from the fruit of the Spirit. A life lived and motivated by the flesh or sinful human nature may put on religious clothes, but one must be vigilant against such self-deception. The Galatians were urged to "live by the Spirit" instead (Galatians 5:16), and such a life would bear true spiritual fruit. Paul listed the fruit in this way: "But the fruit of the Spirit is love, joy, peace, patience, kindness, goodness, faithfulness, gentleness and self-control" (Galatians 5:22-23).

In a day of decreasing biblical literacy in the church, many Christians would not be able to name the nine characteristics in Paul's list of the fruit of the Spirit, let alone explain adequately what they mean. They may vaguely remember some sermons that they may have heard on these verses, but would not have many clues about how these characteristics should be experienced and exhibited in their lives. Those who want to read about them on their own or in Bible study groups may find some useful books, but there are not many.

This book is therefore written to meet a real need in the church. It helps the reader to explore Paul's listing of the fruit of the Spirit by first dealing with some central truths and principles. The fruit of the Spirit can only be well-understood if we recognise its Trinitarian roots — that it has to do with the Father's eternal purpose, the character of the Son of God, and the ministry and power of the indwelling Holy Spirit. The first three chapters of the book deal with this most important truth, which is then woven through the rest of the book. We will also explore the dynamic that lies behind the bearing of the fruit of the Spirit — that it is based on remaining in Christ and being filled with the Holy Spirit.

We will see how virtue is the result of divine grace and our response to it, how God operates within us, and then we are expected to cooperate with Him. Our trust in God and dependence on His grace must be active, which means that we must exercise spiritual discipline to obey Christ and to develop the Christlike character that grows within us as the Spirit fills our hearts. For example, while we experience kindness welling within us, we must find outlets for that kindness in our everyday lives. Like the servants who diligently and faithfully used the talents given by their master (Matthew 25:14-30), we are to use what God gives us. The more we use what is given, the more we will receive and develop the character of Christ in us. We must, therefore, exercise what is given to us.

The fruit of the Spirit is one fruit with nine characteristics, indicating that we cannot have a piecemeal approach to it. It is not a buffet meal where we can pick and choose what we fancy. Rather, it represents one character (the character of Jesus), primarily characterised by love. The various characteristics of the fruit of the Spirit are different expressions of this divine love which is shed abroad in our hearts by the Holy Spirit.

Individual chapters will be devoted to each of the nine characteristics in Paul's list. In each case, our focus will be on the character of God as revealed in Jesus. It is important we keep our eyes on Jesus as we examine each virtue because the fruit of the Spirit really has to do with the character of Jesus. The chapters will therefore be rooted in biblical texts that describe the character of God and Jesus. In addition, throughout the book, the spiritual dynamic has to be understood and experienced. The fruit is the result of the operation of the Holy Spirit within us, which requires our cooperation and spiritual discipline. In each chapter we will also explore how the Spirit's fruit can take shape and grow in our daily lives and relationships.

This book is written so that it can be used both for personal as well as for group study. The questions at the end of each chapter will help readers to further reflect on and explore the topics. I commend this book to the church in the hope that a lost focus can be recovered, and that there would be greater concern and attention given to the nature and dynamic of the truly Spirit-filled life that is rooted and lived in Christ, and the deep changes in our character that accompany such an authentic Christian life.

To God be the glory!

Bishop Robert Solomon
Easter, 2012.

1

THE FATHER'S PURPOSE

There is insufficient attention given to biblical teaching on the fruit of the Holy Spirit and the call to bear the likeness of Jesus Christ because of limited views of biblical salvation. For many people, salvation is merely a change in our final destination. We are on the train to hell; we pray to receive Christ into our hearts and we are instantly changed to another train — the one that is going to heaven. This is true but it does not tell the whole story.

We have to ask what God's purpose is when He saves us. Is it merely, to borrow one popular contemporary slogan, "to plunder hell to populate heaven"? It is clear that God wants everyone to be saved, to fill heaven with all the human beings He has created. Most of us can understand that part of the Father's love. After all, the Bible does say, "The Lord is not slow in keeping his promise, as some understand slowness. He is patient with you, not wanting anyone to perish, but everyone to come to repentance" (2 Peter 3:9).

Salvation takes place when we repent, believe in Jesus and have our sins forgiven. For many that is the sum of salvation. But there is more to it if we read the Bible carefully. For one thing, the Bible does say that God has saved us, is saving us and will save us one day. Salvation took place in the past, is continuing in the present and will culminate in the future. How should we then understand this?

There have been two streams of contributions to Christian theology to help the Church understand Christian salvation. One comes from a legal or forensic perspective, and the other from a medical or therapeutic perspective. Both are needed to help us understand the full implications of the Gospel of Jesus Christ.

Salvation as Forgiveness and the Removal of Guilt

Many major theologians, such as Tertullian, came from a legal background.[1] It is therefore understandable that their legal minds picked up what they were trained to look out for. A lawyer is trained to think in forensic terms. The key question in a legal mind would be, "Is there guilt or not?" It is thus no surprise that these theologians focused on the aspects of salvation that deal with the removal of our guilt.

The Gospel does offer divine forgiveness, a key ingredient of the Good News. We remember the powerful story told by the Lord Jesus of the prodigal son and his gracious and forgiving father (Luke 15:11-32). Though the son had sinned against heaven and his father, the father readily and generously forgave his repentant son, welcoming him home and restoring him to his original status.

It is clear from the Bible that we have all sinned and fallen short of the glory of God (Romans 3:23). The stubborn stain of guilt that we carry in our souls cannot be removed no matter how hard we try, whether through religious piety or attempts to live morally. No degree of good works can succeed in removing this deeply embedded guilt. And because of this guilt, we are all headed for the punishment that awaits those who are carrying this guilt.

Here is where the Gospel steps in. God has offered forgiveness through the sacrifice of His Son Jesus on the cross. The cross of Jesus stands between heaven and earth, offering atonement for our sins, so that through the finished work of Christ, we can be forgiven as we come to God in repentance. As we respond to God with repentance and faith, we are then justified.

Justification is an important Christian doctrine. It is a judicial act of God, declaring us not guilty on the basis of the blood of Jesus shed on the cross (Romans 5:9). Through the grace of God (Titus 3:7) and the blood of Jesus, our sins are forgiven, and our guilt and punishment removed. We are given a new status, that of being the children of God (John 1:12) and we have access to the Father on that basis (Romans 5:1-2).

All this is the wonderful Good News that the Church is tasked to proclaim through its evangelism and mission. The Protestant reformers had rightly emphasised the doctrine of justification by faith in Christ alone. Evangelicals have also laid emphasis on the same. We have nevertheless tended to congregate at the border between the kingdom of light and the kingdom of darkness, calling and urging people to step out from darkness into the glorious light of God's grace and love. When people do cross over, we rejoice together with heaven. But when the new convert asks us about the next steps, we inevitably point to the distant future, to the hazy horizons of heaven. When pressed further, we may present the convert with programmes rather than a spiritual road map to travel to the distant destination. We give vague instructions about the journey ahead, especially as it relates to the inner life.

Salvation as Healing and Transformation

This is where the other major perspective on Christian salvation is important. Besides the forensic or legal perspective, the medical or therapeutic perspective is of utmost importance. Having existed all along in Christian theology, this perspective has been emphasised by theologians and church fathers who had a more medical perspective of things. We must remember that the Greek word *sōzō* used in the New Testament to indicate salvation (e.g. Matthew 1:21), also means "healing." This idea has been developed by the New Testament writers when they talk about sanctification — another key Christian doctrine. This has been particularly emphasised in the eastern branch of Christianity, in the Orthodox traditions. No surprise here, as there was a time when several of the Orthodox bishops were also medical doctors — creating a tradition of physician-bishops. (Interestingly I met an Orthodox bishop from Egypt while studying in Edinburgh University and found that he was also a medical doctor.)

John Wesley, who was greatly influenced by some of the eastern Fathers, picked up the medical view of salvation, and preached and wrote much on this matter. He reminded his listeners and readers that God saves us not only to remove our guilt but also to transform us to become holy and Christlike. Wesley preached sermons like "The First-fruits of the Spirit" where he gave emphasis to the freedom from guilt which we can enjoy through the justification that comes from God. But he also emphasised the need for us to be sanctified and perfected in God's holiness and love.

For example, in his sermon, "The Great Privilege of Those that are Born of God," Wesley preached on the importance of the new birth. While justification and the new birth occur simultaneously, they were not identical events. He said, "Justification implies a change in the relationship between God and human beings. The new birth implies a change in our inward nature. When God justifies us He does something *for us*. When He gives birth to us a second time He does something *within us*. Justification *changes our outward relationship to God* from enmity to friendship, indeed to a father-child relationship. The new birth *changes us inwardly* from being sinners to being saints"[2] (emphasis added).

The medical perspective of salvation sees our human problem not only as (legal) guilt that must be removed so that we can escape punishment. It also sees our problem as a disease. Sin is a disease of the soul which must be healed and removed from our system. We need to become free not only from the *penalty* of sin (justification), but also from the *power* of sin (sanctification). If we travel on this road of salvation offered by God's grace, we can look forward to the day when we can become totally free — even from the *presence* of sin (glorification).

From the medical point of view, the disease of the soul needs to be fixed. The spiritual "treatment" begins with regeneration or the new birth when God gives us a new heart to love and obey Him. We then become new creatures when the old man is buried in baptism and the new man is invited to walk with Christ (Romans 6). In this sense, if justification changes our *standing*, then regeneration changes our *nature* — one changes our status while the other changes our character.

The Christian experience can be compared to medical treatment. Christ is our Divine Physician, who came to deal with sin, the cancer of our souls. He Himself is our medicine, as we receive Him into our lives — a truth which we are regularly reminded of in church whenever we partake of the Lord's Supper. Jesus is the divine medicine and food for our diseased and impoverished souls. As we feed on Him, we become healed and restored, strong and spiritually healthy.

The Church as a Spiritual Hospital

The Church in this perspective is like a spiritual hospital (though it is not only a hospital). Many come to it, some for emergency treatment, others are warded in intensive care, yet others are recuperating in the general wards. We are all being healed and delivered from the deadly disease of sin. Our Divine Physician has appointed some of the patients to assist Him as under-physicians. Their task is to give first-aid and help those who are recovering — to be "healers of the soul" (literally, "psychiatrists" from Greek *psychē* and *iatros*), although increasingly, because they have become busy with lesser duties, their titles have been assumed by secular healers.

The medical perspective helps us to grasp the fuller implications of the salvation that comes from God's gracious hands and loving heart. Without it, we may end up focusing only on the outward aspects of religious piety and fall prey to an activism that is centred on the anxiety that comes from unresolved guilt. Without it, we may never really give adequate attention to the inner man that Paul writes about in Ephesians 3:14-19. Paul's prayer for the Ephesian Christians was that they would be strengthened as the Holy Spirit works in their inner being, so that Christ may dwell in their hearts. As Christ makes our hearts His home, He becomes not only Resident but also President in our hearts. He resides and presides in our lives. As He does so, we begin to plumb the depths of His love, and soar to the heights of His divine goodness. We can then be filled with the fullness of God.

What Does Jesus Do in Our Hearts?

William Holman Hunt's famous painting, *The Light of the World*, shows Christ at the door of our hearts, a wonderful reminder of the work of Christ in our lives as our Divine Physician. He comes in gently with a lamp, and shows us what is wrong in our hearts. Thankfully He does not come in with an overpowering spotlight, otherwise we may die of shock! As Jesus reveals who we are and the true condition of our hearts, and as we obey Him and do what He says, the Divine Physician washes and cleans the festering sores and hidden abscesses of our souls, applying His divine medicine to heal us. This goes on for a lifetime, and one day when the Lord returns in glory, the spotlights will be turned on, and we do not have to be embarrassed or sorry that we had neglected the healing and redemption of our own souls.

There is a great need for the medical perspective to be strengthened in the life, ministry and mission of the church. There is a rich storehouse of treasures in the church, if we search the many spiritual writings that wise and holy Christians have written throughout the history of the church. There are streams of the therapeutic perspective of salvation that have focused on God's secret work in our inner beings, that remind us that God's work in us is as important, if not more important, than God's work through us. The church has identified the deadly sins that lurk within us, and the many masks we wear, including religious ones. We have in our storehouse profound understanding of how God heals us of our sinfulness and brings forth Christlikeness and Christian virtues. We have ways of discerning God's still small voice in the deep recesses of our hearts, of unmasking our own self-deceptive ways, and of developing a deep and intimate relationship with God.

An essential part of the healing of our souls and their restoration to health includes pain and suffering, just as in medical treatment. Unfortunately, in our activist Christian environment, there is little place for suffering and pain in our theology, worship and daily Christian living. We are not willing to undergo God's radical treatment of our condition, or to be "immobilised" and "isolated" in solitude, silence and stillness, so that the Divine Physician can do His healing work (Mark 2:17). We are so much the poorer for running away from His treatment.

On the other hand, if we are to trust Jesus and submit ourselves to His divine therapy, we can become whole again, as He removes the cancer in our soul, binds our inner wounds, and restores us to glowing spiritual health. If we do this, then we will appreciate the healing hands of God touching our diseased souls and the image of Christ forming within us (Galatians 4:19). *This is the mystery of God's salvation and His glory: that Christ is formed in us, and sin is removed forever from our souls.* Thus we are saved and we become first, "Amens" and then we grow into "Alleluias." What begins as the "Amen" of faith is transformed, as a result of the healing of our souls, into the "Alleluia" of glory. This is the purpose of our salvation and our destiny in Christ, the Divine Physician.

God's Purpose for Us

What then is God's purpose for us? He wants to save us from our sins and from our sinful selves, and from death (which is the consequence of our sin). This salvation includes the removal of our guilt through the blood of Jesus so that we are justified before God's judgment seat. It also includes the healing of our souls from our sinful selves. In other words, God wants us to become freed from the penalty of sin, as well as the power of sin, and one day He will free us from the presence of sin.

The Father's purpose is summarised in 1 Peter 1:2 where we read that we "have been chosen according to the foreknowledge of God the Father, through the sanctifying work of the Spirit, for obedience to Jesus Christ and sprinkling by His blood." Salvation includes the "sanctifying work of the Spirit" — a point reiterated by Paul when he wrote, "But we ought always to thank God for you, brothers loved by the Lord, because from the beginning God chose you to be saved through the sanctifying work of the Spirit and through belief in the truth" (2 Thessalonians 2:13). We note here that Paul, in his writings (see, for example 1 Corinthians 6:11; Romans 8:30) brings the whole process of salvation: justification (removal of our guilt), sanctification (victory over sin and growth in holiness), and glorification (sharing in the glory of Christ) under the operation and reality of God's loving grace.

The Grace of God

Theologians have used the words we have just mentioned (justification, sanctification, glorification — words we find in the Bible) to describe the process by which God saves us. We have already discussed justification (the forensic perspective) and sanctification (the medical perspective). This process culminates in participating in the glory of Christ. Paul writes, "For those God foreknew he also predestined to be conformed to the image of his Son, that he might be the firstborn among many brothers and sisters. And those he predestined, he also called; those he called, he also justified; those he justified, he also glorified" (Romans 8:29-30). We must note here again the bringing together of justification, sanctification ("to be conformed to the image of his Son") and glorification into one process of salvation under the sovereign will and gracious purpose of God.

We must recognise that God's role as our Saviour is connected with His role as our Creator. His plans are larger than what we usually imagine. As Creator and Saviour, He is dealing decisively with the angelic and human rebellion against Him and making all things new. He is not just some kindly train driver who is rescuing as many people as possible to get us on the right train (the train to heaven). He is the Maker of heaven and earth who is recreating all that He has created by doing an unimaginably massive and cosmic makeover. We are included in this grand purpose of God. This means that God is not only interested in bringing us to heaven, but also making us fit for life in the new earth and heaven. He is removing our guilt and our tendency to sin while infusing us with His Spirit so that we will become like His Son. "And just as we have borne the likeness of the earthly man, so shall we bear the likeness of the man from heaven" (1 Corinthians 15:49).

This whole process of salvation is supervised and enabled by the grace of God. The Christians in ancient Galatia had some idea of this process but they became confused by false teachers who derailed their faith. They had come to faith in Christ by trusting in Jesus and the grace of God. They also understood that God expected to see evidence of this salvation. This is where they went wrong, for they began to attempt producing good works through their own efforts. Paul challenged their thinking by asking, "Are you so foolish? After beginning with the Spirit, are you now trying to attain your goal by human effort?" (Galatians 3:3). Paul's criticism is not about their goal but their method. That we must grow into holiness is an accepted goal — something that James takes up in his epistle (and there is no conflict between Paul in his epistle to the Galatians and James in his epistle, as some claim to see). What Paul is against is that the Galatian Christians, due to the wrong teaching to which they had become attracted, had resorted to a theology of works. They were "turning back to those weak and miserable principles" (Galatians 3:9) that had enslaved them in a legalistic religion that focused on the performance of outward religious acts.

The Folly of the Galatians

The Galatian Christians, who had started off well by trusting in the grace of God, were now depending on their own strength and strategies to produce holiness and sanctification. As a result they were becoming derailed and losing the true spiritual vitality that comes from the grace of God. They were descending to the old habits of a legalistic and ritualistic religion that focused on religious ceremonies, measuring sanctification by external piety. A life that is cut off from the life-giving Spirit of God and the enabling grace of God will produce *works* of the flesh rather than the *fruit* of the Spirit. It will eventually display the ugliness of human religiosity rather than the beauty of the character of Christ. Paul therefore urges the Galatian Christians to continue where they had begun, living by faith and trusting the grace of God, so that God's purpose of sanctifying them and producing holiness in them would be brought to a good and glorious conclusion.

The Galatians had some idea of the *destination* but they distorted their *method* and were in danger of leaving the journey altogether. Today, we face an even greater danger. Living in an increasingly materialistic and consumer-driven world that thrives on self-gratification, we face the danger of failing to understand God's purpose in saving us. We want an easy ride to heaven (first-class if possible) where we are served and our every need is met. But the journey to heaven is on a path that has to do with denying our self, carrying the cross and following Jesus (Luke 9:23). Why is this so?

The dominant culture does have negative effects on us and provides many obstacles on the path to a fruit-bearing life. Philip Kenneson has pointed out how cultivating each of the fruit of the Spirit encounters obstacles from the dominant culture.[3]

Love — Culture of Market-style Exchanges (the promotion of self-interest and the commodification of everything).

Joy — Culture of Manufactured Desire (the pursuit of the wrong kind of happiness, the false notion that the new is always better and the rise of rampant consumerism).

Peace — Culture of Fragmentation (the compartmentalisation of life, the growth of interest groups and factions, the excessive defence of "rights" and the idea that we need to be protected from one another, and the sanctioning of violence).

Patience — Culture of Productivity (a mechanical view of time, glorifying productivity and the speeding up of life).

Kindness — Culture of Self-sufficiency (the promotion of self-sufficiency and autonomy and the failure to recognise our indebtedness to many for simple things like our daily bread)

Goodness — Culture of Self-help (an over-optimistic view of human goodness and a lack of attention to moral formation).

Faithfulness — Culture of Impermanence (ephemeral changes and disposability).

Gentleness — Culture of Aggression (the fostering of aggression, self-promotion and the pursuit of power).

Self-control —Culture of Addiction (the preoccupation with self and self-gratification).

This means that like salmon, Christians have to swim against the cultural currents to grow into Christlikeness. They have to be intentional in being counter-cultural and biblically-minded, and develop habits of thinking and acting that enable them to withstand strong cultural pressures from the dominant culture.

God's Grand Purpose

Why is the journey to heaven along the path of the cross? It is because God is doing something even as He brings us to heaven. He is doing a total overhaul in our inner beings so that our self is dethroned and the true King of our lives can be enthroned. He is ridding us of our idols and addictions, of our sinfulness and rebellion. This will often entail suffering, deprivation, pain and loss on our part. But all this is part of God's larger purpose of making a new heaven and earth, and of making a new people who will live in them.

C. S. Lewis uses a metaphor to explain this process. Borrowing an idea from George MacDonald, Lewis writes:

> "Imagine yourself as a living house. God comes in to rebuild that house. At first, perhaps, you can understand what He is doing. He is getting the drains right and stopping the leaks in the roof and so on: you knew that those jobs needed doing and so you are not surprised. But presently He starts

> knocking the house about in a way that hurts abominably and does not seem to make sense. What on earth is He up to? The explanation is that He is building quite a different house from the one you thought of — throwing out a new wing here, putting on an extra floor there, running up towers, making courtyards. You thought you were going to be made into a decent little cottage: but He is building a palace. He intends to come and live in it Himself."[4]

This means that if we see salvation only as getting off scot-free in a cosmic court and getting a one-way ticket to heaven, we are missing a large part of God's purpose and plan. It would be like what happens sometimes — we get into a lift and no one presses the buttons but everyone thinks they are moving up, only to realise embarrassingly that they have been on the same floor all along. They did not move anywhere even though they thought they were moving.

Only as we realise the extent of God's purposes can we then allow God to complete the work that He began in us when we first turned to Him in faith (Philippians 1:6). Only then can we begin to understand the place of pain and suffering in our lives. Only then can we focus on God's work in us and allow Him to change us to be like Jesus. Only then can we bear the fruit of the Holy Spirit and be prepared to live as citizens of the new heaven and earth.

Questions for Reflection

1. Read 1 Peter 1:1-2. What does this passage tell us about God's purposes for us? How would you appropriate this truth for yourself and what difference would it make in the way you are living now?

2. How would you define these terms: salvation, justification, sanctification, glorification? Why are there inadequate or distorted ideas of salvation among Christians? How can this be rectified?

3. "This whole process of salvation is supervised and enabled by the grace of God." What do you understand by this sentence? Read Galatians and discuss what the basic problem of the church was. What similarities can you find in the modern church?

4. How important is the fruit of the Spirit in relation to the purposes of God? How important is this fruit in His purpose for you personally?

2

THE CHARACTER OF JESUS

God's purpose in saving us is to make us like His Son Jesus Christ. In his last book, written just before his death, John Stott shares about the question that perplexed him and his friends as young Christians: What is God's purpose for His people? Stott mentions the great answers given in the Shorter Westminster Catechism — "Man's chief end is to glorify God and to enjoy him for ever" — and the brief statement of the summary of the Law — "Love God, love your neighbour" as good answers but he was not totally satisfied with them. He found that neither the Calvinist doxological (high view of God's glory) perspective nor the Arminian focus on how we ought to be living in response to God were fully satisfying in themselves. With reference to both perspectives, he wrote:

> "But neither seemed to be wholly satisfactory. So I want to share with you where my mind has come to rest as I approach the end of my pilgrimage on earth. It is this: *God wants his people to become like Christ*, for Christlikeness is the will of God for the people of God"[1] (emphasis added).

Stott found his answer to the question about God's purpose for us in Christ. His answer had Christological foundations, and in it he found restful satisfaction that makes the answer theologically clear and pastorally sound. Or to put it another way, as Eugene Peterson has said it, the goal for Christians is God's work of salvation and the means is Jesus.[2]

What does it mean when we say that we are to be like Jesus? The most superficial answer arises from thinking in physical terms, but we instinctively know that that answer is not a satisfactory one, neither reflecting what God has in mind nor mindful of practical realities. It is for this reason perhaps, that we have little information on the physical appearance of Jesus. People have painted the face of Jesus from devotional and intuitive imagination — often leading to Jesus looking like a westerner, a fact that has increasingly been criticised by non-westerners, among whom some have painted Jesus to look like one of their own kind.

We have, of course, various theories of the Turin shroud which purportedly portrays the face of Jesus. Some scientists have even attempted to reconstruct the face of Jesus from the shroud and claim to have produced an image that looks like a first-century Jew. Lest we get too excited about it, we must calmly remember that Scripture is quite silent about how Jesus looked physically — all for good reason I think.

The Invisible God

The human curiosity in desiring to see how God looks like is regularly denied and disappointed in Scripture. Moses, just like many of us, wanted to see God and requested to be shown the glory of the Lord, but God told him, "you cannot see my face, for no one may see me and live" (Exodus 33:18-20). God, as a concession, allowed Moses to have a look at His *back* but not His face as He passed by Moses. Why was God reluctant to show His face?

We get a clue when we note that this event is recorded in Exodus soon after the tragic story of the golden calf, The Israelites, tired of waiting for Moses to come down from Mount Sinai, had built a divine mascot — a golden calf to accompany them in their journey to the promised land. Moses angrily broke the tablets containing the Ten Commandments when he saw what was happening. What we see here is a conflict between the religion of the eye (idolatry) and the religion of the ear (reading and hearing the Law). This conflict is woven in throughout the Old Testament and continues in the New Testament too.

True biblical religion is based on hearing God rather than seeing God's appearance. There is a constant warning that any attempt to "peek" at God would have fatal results. There is also a strong warning against representing God in some particular form, for such attempts would result in idolatry — seeing God in a way that reduces Him to an object conceived by human minds and made by human hands. God is the wholly Other, and the only way we can truly perceive Him is by listening to Him. In other words, the biblical God is an audible God rather than a visible God. We may see the effects of God's presence (in the case of the contemporaries of Moses, it included a cloud-covered quaking mountain), but God Himself remains invisible to human eyes. God is to be perceived by the ears more than the eyes.

Jesus Makes God Visible

We encounter something radical when we come to Jesus. While we read that He is the *logos* (Word) of God (John 1:1-2) — and that ties in nicely with the truth that God is primarily heard rather than seen — we are also told that "The Word became flesh and made his dwelling among us" (John 1:14). God became visible for a moment in history in the Incarnation. Hence, Jesus declared, "When a man believes in me, he does not believe in me only, but in the one who sent me. *When he looks at me, he sees the one who sent me*" (John 12:44-45, emphasis added).

Before He went to the cross, Jesus had a number of significant conversations with His disciples who had been with Him for more than three years. He told them how He was going to die but reassured them of His presence through the Holy Spirit. One of the disciples, Philip, told Jesus with little understanding, "Lord, show us the Father and that will be enough for us" (John 14:8). Jesus expressed His disappointment in the answer He gave. "Don't you know me, Philip, even after I have been among you such a long time? *Anyone who has seen me has seen the Father.* How can you say, 'Show us the Father'? Don't you believe that I am in the Father, and that the Father is in me?" (John 14:9-10, emphasis added). Jesus was not only God made audible but also God made visible.

Thus we are not surprised when Paul and the writer of Hebrews declared Jesus to be the image (*eikōn*) of God. In Paul's words, Jesus "is the image of the invisible God" (Colossians 1:15), a truth that is echoed in the opening words of Hebrews: "The Son is the radiance of God's glory and the exact representation of his being" (Hebrews 1:3). Jesus was not an idol of God but the perfect image (*eikōn*) of God. He was both God audible and God visible, *logos* and *eikōn*.

An idol is something (less than God) made to represent God. When idolatry occurs, the nature and character of God is diminished, distorted and dishonoured — hence the strong prohibition in Scripture against idolatry. The created cannot represent God. Only the uncreated can represent the uncreated. This is why the Incarnation is both uniquely stupendous and mysteriously unique. Jesus, Scripture testifies, is God Himself (John 20:28; 1 Timothy 3:16; Titus 2:13; Hebrews 1:8-9). In the Incarnation, the invisible God is made visible for a moment in history, so that all who see Him and believe would, instead of experiencing death, live and receive eternal life. (He will be made visible again at the end of history and for all eternity.)

The Character of God

What was it about God that was made visible in Jesus? We have already noted that Scripture says hardly anything about the appearance of Jesus. If His physical appearance is meant to be significant to us, Scripture would have focused on it. Even Philip who saw and spoke to Jesus did not catch the point readily — that Jesus made God visible in His character. Jesus showed how God would be if He became a man. In so doing, Jesus not only became the perfect Man who was sacrificed on the cross for our redemption, but He has also become the gold standard for all human beings. He is the perfect example of godliness — of what we would be when God takes residence in our hearts.

Scripture is interested in telling its readers about the identity and character of Jesus, and not about His physical appearance. We would understand this if we remember the dangers of the religion of the eye and the limitations and destructiveness of idolatry. Therefore when we read the Bible, we encounter the character of Jesus in all that is said about Him. When we read about Jesus, whether in the narrative accounts in the Gospels, or in the didactic doctrinal and pastoral sections in the epistles, we are informed about who Jesus is — His identity and character. This should then be our focus when we read Scripture.

The apostles, who saw Jesus face to face, made it clear in their teaching and preaching about Jesus, that their focus was not on the physical appearance of Jesus but on His identity (as Son of God, Messiah and Saviour of the world) and character (the very character of God Himself). This is why we still remember who He was rather than how He looked. Even the early hymns (of which Philippians 2:5-11 is believed by scholars to be one) reflect this focus.

The Character of Jesus in the Gospels

How, then, can we determine what the character of Jesus was from the biblical record we have today? The most significant part of Scripture in this regard is the section called the Gospels. There are four Gospels all containing narrative accounts of Jesus. They are not biographies as we understand them today. The Gospels are not a diary-like record of the chronological events in the life of Jesus. There are many missing parts, with minimal information on Jesus' childhood and young adulthood.

That is not surprising because the aim of the Gospels is to present Jesus in terms of His identity, character and mission. This becomes evident in what He said and did, and the circumstances surrounding His life, many of which were the fulfilment of earlier prophecies in Scripture. The Gospels contain narratives and in them was theology

— both doctrinal and pastoral — such as the triune nature of God, Christ as God and man, the atonement, the cross, how to live a godly life and how to handle suffering.

We would do well if we read the Gospels more slowly so that we not only end up with information about Jesus, but we have a growing knowledge and understanding about His identity and character. We see in the Gospels not only doctrinal teaching but also a demonstration of what it means to live by every word that proceeds from the mouth of God, and what is involved in seeking the Kingdom of God and its righteousness above all that the world offers. We discover how godliness encounters temptation, how a godly man should relate with people (with righteousness, compassion and courage). We usually miss these things when we read the Gospels merely for information or as nothing more than a moral text (that we should live according to some principles and rules).

Encountering Jesus

When we learn to read the Gospels more deeply, we will encounter the Person of Jesus Christ. The more we behold and relate with Him — the more we have a chance of becoming like Him. The more we learn to walk with Him, the more we can reflect His character in our daily lives. A slower and more contemplative way of reading the Gospels was devised by Ignatius of Loyola in what has become the Ignatian method of reading the Gospels. This involves using the senses to get into the stories and narratives found in the Gospels so that we are not just readers but become participants. We do not just read about Jesus but are led to encounter Him. Such methods help us to understand the importance of reading the Gospels in order to encounter Jesus. How else can we walk with Jesus? How else can we know something about the character of Jesus except by reflecting slowly and meditatively on what Scripture says about Him?

Our encounter with Jesus must be based on Scripture and not on our imaginations about Him. The more we read Scripture carefully and reflectively, the greater the chance we have of reflecting the character of Jesus. This is an important dimension of Christian discipleship.

We need to have the experience of Bill Donahue who wrote a book about keeping company with Jesus "to reveal Jesus as we encounter him in the stories of the Bible – on walks, at dinner, in the marketplace, on a hillside",[3] never ceasing to be amazed at these encounters. Donahue shares:

> "For twenty-three years I have been like Zachaeus in the Bible, watching Jesus from the branches of a sycamore tree. And then, just like in the story, he called my name, 'Bill! Bill Donahue! Come down here. I want to hang out with you today!' I leapt from the tree and began a journey in the company of Jesus and those who follow his ways.
>
> Along the way I have discovered that you do not have just one encounter with Jesus. Each time you meet him the encounter is fresh and engaging. It adds texture and colour to the relationship. You are unnerved by what he says, startled by what he does and confused by what he seems to be. On some occasions you feel you have much in common with this man from Galilee, yet moments later you are overwhelmed by his greatness and feel grateful to simply stand in the shadow of his robe."[4]

We read about the character of Jesus not only in the Gospels, but also in the Epistles (most of which were in fact written before the Gospels). A representative list would illustrate this.

Humility. The classic text is the ancient hymn in Philippians 2:5-11. Paul urges us to have the mind and attitude of Christ, which was characterised by humility and willing, wholehearted obedience. "Your attitude should be the same as that of Jesus Christ...he humbled himself and became obedient to death" (Philippians 2:5,8).

Meekness and gentleness. "By the meekness and gentleness of Christ, I appeal to you..." (2 Corinthians 10:1).

Generosity. "For you know the grace of our Lord Jesus Christ, that though he was rich, yet for your sakes he became poor, so that you through his poverty might become rich" (2 Corinthians 8:9).

Love. "Be imitators of God, therefore, as dearly loved children, and live a life of love, just as Christ loved us and gave himself up for us, as a fragrant offering and sacrifice to God" (Ephesians 5:1-2). Paul's well-known and most beautiful description of godly love in 1 Corinthians 13 is a portrayal of the very character of Jesus. Each of the statements about love in that passage can be exemplified by something said about Jesus in the Gospels.

Forgiveness. "Forgive as the Lord forgave you" (Colossians 3:13).

Perseverance. "May the Lord direct your hearts into God's love and Christ's perseverance" (2 Thessalonians 3:5).

The above list is obviously not comprehensive for there is a lot more said in the epistles about the character of Jesus, from which we get an idea of the person of Jesus. Suffice to say, we are challenged to read the Bible more carefully so that we will encounter Jesus and discover His identity and character more deeply. We are encouraged to recognise that Jesus has left us an example (especially in His sufferings for us) and to "follow in his steps" (1 Peter 2:21).

The Character of Christ and Fruit of the Spirit

The fruit of the Spirit described by Paul in Galatians 5:22-23 is in fact the character of Jesus. All the various virtues listed by Paul are perfectly found and displayed in Jesus as described in Scripture. We find each of them (love, joy, peace, patience, kindness, goodness, faithfulness, gentleness and self-control) displayed fully in the life of Christ. For example, Jesus displayed the greatest love — the self-giving kind — at the cross when He exchanged places with sinful humankind. He showed self-control when tempted by Satan to turn stones into bread to feed His hungry body.

There are two errors we must avoid when thinking about the fruit of the Spirit.

Firstly, we must not intentionally or unintentionally separate the fruit of the Holy Spirit from the character of Jesus. That would be a failure to understand the nature of the triune God and the way He functions. The fruit of the Spirit is not something that we develop or build by seeking some esoteric spiritual experience. Neither is it something that we can make within ourselves by following some strategy or programme. The fruit of the Spirit has to do with studying and reflecting the character of Christ by allowing Him to live in and through us by the power of the Holy Spirit.

We are filled with Christ when we are filled by the Holy Spirit. We are likewise filled by the Spirit when we are filled by Christ. Both are similar experiences because the Holy Spirit is mentioned in several places in the New Testament as the Spirit of Jesus (Acts 16:7; Romans 8:9; Galatians 4:6; Philippians 1:19, 1 Peter 1:11). This means that when we are full of the Holy Spirit we will display a good measure of the character of Jesus — which we call the fruit of the Spirit. The role of the Holy Spirit in this process is of utmost importance. This is explored more closely in chapter three.

We must bear in mind that the Holy Spirit must not be separated from the Person and character of Jesus. It is unfortunate that the three Persons in the Trinity are often separated in popular Christian thinking and practice. When we separate and dissociate the Spirit from Jesus, we are in danger of distorting what Scripture teaches. (Similar dangers exist when dissociations are created between the Spirit and the Word, or the Spirit and the church).

In practice, and for the purposes of our study, we must reiterate that the bearing of the fruit of the Spirit has a lot to do with the study of the Word, especially in terms of the Person and character of Jesus Christ, and walking with this Christ and walking in His steps. This is not the whole story, for it involves what Scripture calls living "in Christ" so that Christ also lives in us and is shown forth in our lives. As a result our character takes on His character as we study, surrender to, and obey Jesus. We will discuss this in greater detail in the next chapter. For now, it suffices to say that part of this process involves reading and reflecting on what Scripture reveals about the character of Jesus. There is enough there for us to practice this for a lifetime.

We are called to walk as Jesus walked (1 John 2:6) and must reflect on what this involves and how it becomes reality in our lives. Much of it depends on keeping our eyes on Jesus. When we turn away from Jesus, we will lose our way. Each quality or virtue found in Paul's list of the fruit of the Spirit is best understood in connection with the life of Christ. The practice of these virtues, as George Maloney points out, "is a true participation in the nature of Christ."[3]

One more thing needs to be said here. When we look at Paul's list of Spirit-cultivated virtues, we will at some point encounter the issue of culture. Does gentleness look one way to Japanese Christians and another way to their American brethren? Can culture create differences in the way we expect virtues like gentleness to be expressed? Elsewhere I have dealt with issues related to cultural differences in our understanding of Christian virtues.[4]

I recall that when I was studying in Edinburgh University, there were students from many parts of the world. Some new Indian students shared with me that the Scottish Christians were a rather unfriendly lot and they were disturbed by it. They explained that they were in Scotland and a few Scottish Christians visited them only once and then left them alone. They considered this to be a cold and perfunctory form of hospitality. I realised that in their culture hospitality was given and received in more intensive ways. Local hosts would visit guests frequently, plan everything for them, and feel that any unattended space and time would be a sign of lapses in hospitality.

On the other hand, a westerner may find such hospitality to be smothering and overbearing — with the hosts breathing down their neck and not allowing them space and freedom to do their own things. We can understand why the Scots who thought they were discreetly hospitable (in their respect for privacy and personal space) were not appreciated by the Indians whose ideas of hospitality were quite different.[5]

Similar differences can be noted when we think of patience and kindness and many of the other virtues. Some cultures would consider it quite normal to spend half a day in a post office or government office when in another culture the tolerance level would be much more limited. When does someone become impatient? Kindness in one culture may mean dropping everything you are doing to walk a mile with someone who is lost and asking for directions. In another culture it may simply mean giving verbal directions.

With cultural differences to consider, it is important that we have a common reference point — Jesus Christ. Jesus was a real person who walked on earth 2,000 years ago. His words, actions and relationships are recorded for us in Scripture. He offers us a living picture that can help us — no matter what culture we belong to — to take our bearing and find a model that can be widely applied in all cultures. In this respect, the Holy Spirit incarnates Christ in individuals and cultures. We are not dealing with theoretical or philosophical constructs but a real Person who is incarnated in the lives of His followers in all cultures. Jesus is the Man for all seasons and all cultures.

The second error when studying the fruit of the Spirit is to have such a piecemeal approach that we miss the whole point. To begin with, Paul's list of nine virtues is generally understood by scholars as not comprehensive or complete. We cannot go away thinking that this list gives the whole picture about the character of Christ. However, though not comprehensive, an adequate study of Paul's list will give a pretty good picture of the character of Jesus. Therefore, though the list does not include some of the historically articulated key Christian virtues such as hope, courage and justice, they can be found to be in relation to different virtues in Paul's list in Galatians. For example, it is quite easily understood that to live in faithfulness, one will have to live courageously when facing the consequences of remaining faithful to God.

The problem arises when the list is dissected to leave us with an impersonal list of virtues (unconnected with Jesus who enfleshed them in His life) or when we are led to think in a fragmented way that one can pick and choose one or more of these virtues to work on at the expense of the others. Can one be gentle and not practice self-control? Can one be patient and not be faithful?

The point is that the virtues make sense only when they are seen  together as a whole. Thus interestingly Paul commits an intentional grammatical "error" to make an essential theological point. Instead of using the plural "fruits" to describe the nine characteristics in his list, Paul used the singular "fruit." The Holy Spirit's fruit is singular; it comes as a single cluster of various qualities. Some have compared this to the way the colours of the rainbow are all derived from a single source of light.

We have a single fruit of the Holy Spirit because it points to the singular character of Jesus Christ. This leads us to various practical pointers. In the first place, our focus should be on the character of Jesus as the overall theme rather than on Paul's list as a list of disparate qualities — a smorgasbord from which we can happily pick and choose what we like or are inclined towards. In the second place, the fruit of the Spirit reflects the wholesome character of Jesus. It is not a fragmented list of virtues. Like the pieces of a jigsaw puzzle, the virtues help to build a more complete picture that makes sense. Or better still, they are like the colours in a painting that together build up a portrait. If we pick only a few colours we may most likely fail to see the portrait.

Bearing this portrait in mind prevents us from a fragmented approach that takes us away from the real purpose of thinking about the fruit of the Spirit. To put it differently, the various virtues in Paul's list are to be understood only in terms of our relationship with Jesus. When we relate with Jesus, we come into contact with His character. It is His character (by the sanctifying actions of the Holy Spirit) that we will display in our lives — and this will show the various qualities listed by Paul.

We move from the whole to the parts, and not the other way round. We cannot hope to engage in some psychological techniques at self-management, self-improvement or self-talk and thereby build up the virtues listed by Paul. The secret has to do more with relationship than with theoretical knowledge, one of surrender to the Lordship of Jesus rather than a set of self-improvement techniques (no matter how spiritual they sound). This we will explore in the next chapter.

We must make three final points before moving to the next chapter. First, the *character of Christ is for the individual as well as for the community.* The individual Christian is to exhibit the very character of Christ. But this is intimately connected to how the church, the body of Christ, corporately expresses the character of Christ. In its worship, ministry, relationships, service, attitudes, and in so many other ways, the church is challenged to reflect the very character of Jesus. This is emphasised in Philip Kenneson's book that focuses on cultivating the Spirit's fruit in *Christian community.*[6] He provides useful pointers on how the church's worship, fellowship, nurture and priorities can help to cultivate the various aspects of the fruit of the Spirit. This is an important point to bear in mind — that the church should be a Christlike community if it is to nurture Christlike people.

Second, *developing and nurturing a community of Christian virtue is not an easy task today.* Theologian David Wells has shown how three major shifts in popular culture have taken place in our time that would make it difficult to focus on virtue and character.[7] Firstly, there is the shift from virtues (universally held, normative concepts of goodness) to values (personal preferences "that are thought about in an ironically value-free way"). Secondly, a shift has taken place from placing emphasis on character to personality. Character can be thought of in moral terms (good and bad) while personality is thought of in functional terms (healthy and unhealthy). Thirdly, the focus has shifted linguistically from "human nature" to "self." Wells describes a consumer paradise for the modern self:

> "In this paradise, there is no moral constraint or need for moral discrimination. Here, in this land, heaven and hell have contracted into the small flashes of pleasure or the daily bumps of pain that become our lot and nothing more. Here, we experience ourselves as selves who can be remade, selves whose desire must be satiated, selves whose uniqueness and whose pleasures, pains or perplexities, are matters to be revealed before any audience, large or small, indeed, anyone willing to hear. God has receded into the far-off distance; and human nature is now part of a forgotten language, one we have no interest in recovering."[8]

Wells' description rings true in terms of how modern people live their lives today as they are shaped by popular ideologies, mantras and lifestyles promoted by the market and media. Sadly, these influences have infected the church so that today many church-goers are looking for personal happiness more than holiness. They come as religious consumers more than as responsible members of a loving and moral community. It is in this context that the church has to demonstrate that it is a Christ-centred godly community which lives in the redemptive story of Christ and demonstrates His character in its life, witness and interactions. This has to be done in the way it worships, ministers, nurtures faith (especially in the young), conducts Bible-study, promotes deep and godly relationships, and serves the community.

Third, as our Lord has shown, *the building of Christian character is a process that has much to do with the suffering that comes by walking on the way of the cross.* Calvin Miller asks, "Character: what is it? What we are on the inside? What our mother thinks we are? What we are in the dark?" and answers, "No, only this: What we will be when the finished work of Christ is added to our unyielding desire to live for his pleasure."[9] In his answer, Miller directs our attention to the heart of our motives. Only a total commitment to Jesus will do if we are serious about being perfected into the character of Christ. Miller points out that "the time when we best develop character is when we are no longer in charge of our circumstances. To be under the heel of someone else's will or to suffer the indignity of crushing circumstances, these incarcerations of body give wings to the spirit."[10]

If we are serious about growing into Christlikeness, we must expect suffering and setbacks allowed by God not to punish us but to shape and strengthen us, to mould our character into permanent shape. It is thus more important when we pray, not to ask for our uncomfortable circumstances to change, but for God to shape our character. We often get our prayers wrong because we do not understand the ways of God or His purposes. But can we withstand the onslaught of suffering along the way? Should we grit our teeth and stoically bear it? This is where we need to reflect on the inner resources and spiritual springs God has provided. In our own strength, we cannot walk on the way of the cross. We will naturally quit and run away. But the Spirit of Jesus strengthens and enables us to remain on the way of the cross so that we will become transformed into Christlikeness even as we faithfully walk on it.

Questions for Reflection

1. Do you agree with John Stott when he asserts that the key purpose of God is for us to become Christlike? How can this become a conviction and a life goal for Christians?

2. Read the section in the chapter where some of the characteristics of Jesus are portrayed in Scripture and look up the scripture references. Can you think of other character qualities of Jesus that can be added to the list?

3. Discuss the two errors mentioned in the chapter that must be avoided. Why is it important that our understanding of the fruit of the Spirit must be firmly grounded in the character of Jesus Christ?

4. What daily implications are there for a disciple of Jesus who is committed to "walk as Jesus did" (1 John 2:6)?

3

THE FRUIT OF THE SPIRIT

Paul's list of Christian virtues in Galatians has to do with the purposes of the Father in heaven (as we discussed in chapter 1). They also have to do with the character of His Son Jesus Christ (as we saw in chapter 2). In this chapter we focus on the truth that the list has to do with the Holy Spirit — it is the fruit of the Spirit.

We cannot attain the character of Christ simply by training ourselves or by attending some "how-to" course. It cannot be manufactured by self-effort. It is in essence supernatural rather than natural in process and result.

This brings us to an age-old question about how God's grace operates. Are we saved by waiting or by self-effort? The Protestant point was that we are saved by the grace of God and not by our religious works. As some old preachers used to preach, the basic gospel message is not "do" but "done." It is not "do this" and "do that" but "trust in Jesus and you will be saved." All this is true, for the Bible does tell us that our best efforts at holiness fail miserably. It tells us colourfully and without mincing words that "all our righteous acts are like filthy rags" (Isaiah 64:6).

The Futile Way of the Pharisees

Another way of looking at it is to say that we have to be perfect to be in heaven, for heaven is a perfect place for perfect people. Jesus

Himself said that if one were to please God one has to obey every one of God's rules, with no exception (Matthew 5:12-20). He further urged, "Be perfect, therefore, as your heavenly Father is perfect" (Matthew 5:48). The religion of the Pharisees followed this method of pleasing God, but in the process they tended to focus on outward and visible religious acts — acts that can be arithmetically measured and kept as an accounting record. But God goes deeper than that in examining us.

The Pharisees were obsessed with religiously technical obedience. They practised giving their tithes to the smallest detail; they even tithed their spices and took pride in their religious scrupulosity (Matthew 23:23). They fixed certain rules about the Sabbath. They could only walk a certain maximum distance or carry a certain maximum weight in order not to break the Sabbath. They took obsessive care to ensure that they remained technically perfect in God's sight and enforced this neurotically obsessive religion on their fellow men.

Jesus called them hypocrites and whitewashed tombs (Matthew 23:25-27). They may have failed to acknowledge it but what they appeared to be on the outside did not match what they were on the inside. "You are like whitewashed tombs, which look beautiful outside but on the inside are full of dead men's bones and everything unclean" (Matthew 23:27). This was not surprising because the focus of the Pharisees was fatally in the wrong place. Their religion was one of performance. "Everything they do is done for men to see" (Matthew 23:5).

Trying to save ourselves by our religious works will bring us on the self-deceptive path of the pathetic Pharisees. The basic problem is that we can regulate and modify our outward behaviour and pious acts, but we cannot do anything about what lies inside us. As the ancient prophet asked, "Can the leopard change its spots?" (Jeremiah 13:23). The answer to that rhetorical question is "no." We can change our religious performance but we cannot change our sinful nature and what is within us. Therefore, religious works cannot save us because they cannot make us perfect. We must turn to something (or rather Someone) else if we want to be saved.

The Fruitful Way of the Spirit

The good news is that God has promised to make us fit for heaven. In His grace, at our baptism, we are declared to be children of God (a new status that enables us to be ready for heaven) and clothed with Christ (Galatians 3:26). Paul reminded the Galatian Christians of this truth which they had accepted by faith and therefore had been converted. They had begun in faith and believed that we "wear" Jesus and His perfect righteousness.

Our own righteousness, as we were reminded by Isaiah, can at best look like old filthy rags. How can we then enter the wedding banquet in these old and miserable clothes? But God in His grace and mercy has now clothed us with something that allows us to gain entry — for we will be judged not based on our own grossly inadequate righteousness but on the perfect righteousness of Christ. This is the great doctrine of justification by faith — a doctrine that was stoutly defended by Paul (in his various epistles, especially to the Romans and Galatians) and others in the history of the church. It was also a doctrine that brought real peace and new life to countless men and women (think of Martin Luther, John Wesley, and the like) who had stopped trying to be righteous in their own strength but found salvation through the rest that Christ offers (Matthew 11:28).

The Galatian Confusion

Paul reiterated this great doctrine when he wrote to the Galatians who had accepted it and found new life in Christ. But a serious problem developed in their church when false teachers came to confuse them with a teaching that focused on a theology of works. Our salvation depends on our religious works, they claimed. As part of their teaching, they insisted that besides believing in Christ, they had to practise circumcision to keep the law of God — only then could they be saved. Such dangerous teachings would lead the Christians away from grace and into a deadening legalism that would self-construct one's own salvation. In essence it was a do-it-yourself religion — an old and yet ever-present religion in the human race, one that had distorted the revelation in the Old Testament.

Seeing that the Galatian Christians were in great spiritual danger, Paul pleads with them, "You were running a good race. Who cut in on you and kept you from obeying the truth?" (Galatians 5:7). They faced the danger of building a new (but in reality the same old, tired) theology of works. They would then end up trying to do good works, not out of gratitude to God for His extraordinary and unmerited grace, but to earn their salvation. They were on the old road of the Pharisees.

We must note the key points that Paul makes, for they point to the truth that the Christian life is a supernatural life — lived in Christ and empowered by the Holy Spirit. This is made possible by the grace of God, from beginning till the end.

The Great Secret

The secret of the victorious and virtuous Christian life is found in the sentence: "God sent the Spirit of his Son into our hearts" (Galatians 4:6). Not only is this initiative and enterprise of God Trinitarian in nature, it is also a supernatural experience. We cannot live the Christian life by our own strength. The new dynamic is the Spirit of Christ residing in us and enabling us to please God. The sinful flesh is at odds with the Spirit and will resist the work of the Spirit in our souls.

The problem with a theology and religion of works is that it will bring to the fore the flesh. The flesh is the operating principle in our attempts to please God with our own strength and spirituality. Hence Paul warns that the route the Galatians seemed to have chosen will lead to disaster. He lists the works of the flesh or the sinful nature. "The acts of the flesh are obvious: sexual immorality, impurity and debauchery; idolatry and witchcraft; hatred, discord, jealousy, fits of rage, selfish ambition, dissensions, factions and envy; drunkenness, orgies, and the like. I warn you, as I did before, that those who live like this will not inherit the kingdom of God" (Galatians 5:19-21). This is where the false religion that the Galatians were attracted to would lead them. In other words, while they came out from the highway of wickedness when they accepted Jesus by faith, now they faced the danger of returning to that same old highway.

Paul therefore insists that old outward religious rules such as circumcision amount to nothing significant; "what counts is a new creation" (Galatians 6:15). God's work in us is a spiritual act of regenerating us through the Holy Spirit. When we believe and are baptised we enter into a new spiritual experience, born of the Spirit and living in Christ. The Spirit teaches us to call God "Abba" and "Father" as we learn to understand and appropriate our new and eternal identity as the children of God. We are not like zoo animals being taught to behave and to entertain others with our antics. No, we are sinners who are made into God's children by the supernatural power of the Spirit.

The Spirit helps us to live as God's children by teaching and enabling us to live in Christ. This is a mystery — something that we find in the way Paul describes his calling. "But when God, who set me apart from birth and called me by his grace, was pleased to *reveal his Son in me* so that I might preach him among the Gentiles..." (Galatians 1:15-16, emphasis added). Paul admitted to being somewhat of a religious prodigy ("I was advancing in Judaism beyond many Jews of my own age") and an "extremely zealous" product of Judaism (Galatians 1:14). But he had greatly misunderstood the dynamic of the spiritual life that God had revealed to the Jews, which is not surprising, considering the fact that Paul was a Pharisee, the most religious of the Jews of his day.

Only after he met the risen Christ did Paul begin to understand the real dynamic of the spiritual life. Paul saw the key place that God's sovereignty and grace had in this new spiritual journey that he had embarked on. And at the heart of God's calling was His plan to "reveal His Son in me." In the course of living the Christian life, the Son will increasingly become revealed in us. And this is made possible by the sanctifying work of the Holy Spirit. This is the secret of the true dynamic of the spiritual life.

This is achieved through three experiences on our part: surrender, obedience, and the bearing of spiritual fruit.

Surrender

The Christian life begins with surrender — not by trying to be good or by performing religious acts. When we come to the end of the rope and realise our utter helplessness to save ourselves, like a drowning man, we surrender to the rescuer who comes to save us from certain death. The rescuer will be able to help us when we surrender to his efforts to save us but will have great difficulty if we still thrash about in the water to save ourselves.

Likewise we surrender to God's grace and actions when we come to Christ. What we begin with, we must continue in it to make further progress. This was Paul's point in Galatians. *Christian maturity does not come with self-effort, but by continuing surrender to the rule of Christ and the work of the Spirit within us.* Alas, the sinful nature (flesh) will sabotage such attempts. Not only is it active when one is openly sinning, but it is dangerously and subversively active when we try to be religious. As we have seen earlier, religion does not get rid of the sinful self or put it out of action. For that to happen, we need to understand and submit to the new dynamic of the spiritual life, and "live by the Spirit." We can do so if we submit to the rule of Christ by dying to the sinful self. "Those who belong to Christ Jesus have crucified the sinful nature with its passions and desires" (Galatians 5:24).

Paul describes this process further: "I have been crucified with Christ and *I no longer live*, but *Christ lives in me*" (Galatians 2:20, emphasis added). As we submit to Christ and the leading of the Holy Spirit, the life of Jesus will begin to be displayed in increasing measure so that, more and more, others will see Jesus in us. How will they see this in us?

Living a surrendered life of faith is the underlying reality of the fruit-bearing life of the Spirit.

Obedience

Many people have a rather passive (and unhelpful) view of the surrendered life. They see it as not doing anything but perpetually waiting for God to do His work. The discipline of waiting is important in the Christian life, especially in our increasingly impatient, quick-fix, restless, activist, modern culture. We expect God to work quickly (and often magically — which is not the same as miraculous). Our terms of reference for Christian spirituality may be distorted by our ideas of efficient factory production lines or cash machines. God's methods are often like the ways of cultivation and farming. It takes time and we need to wait. Indeed, as Paul wrote, God is the one who "makes things grow" (1 Corinthians 3:7).

However, farmers cannot afford to do nothing in their farms and claim that since God gives the growth they are excused from all efforts. John Wesley resisted such ideas in his time by arguing for a robust Christianity that was disciplined. *As God operates, we are called to cooperate with Him.*

This truth was taken up by Paul when he wrote "*continue to work out your salvation* with fear and trembling, for *it is God who works in you* to will and to act in order to fulfill his good purpose" (Philippians 2:12-13, NIV, emphasis added). God is at work in us — that is the foundational reality of having Jesus in our hearts and the Holy Spirit residing and working within us. In our own strength we will never be able to please God or become in any way like Jesus. But through the powerful sanctifying work of the Holy Spirit within us, we can grow into Christlikeness as the Spirit enables us to obey God in the way Jesus obeyed His Father.

Within this reality of God's sovereign power working within us, we are also urged to "work out your salvation with fear and trembling." We are called to do our part — which is to submit to God and obey Him, to cooperate with God even as He enables us to do so. According to Paul's Galatian epistle, we are not to give up doing good but continue doing good to all people (Galatians 6:9-10).

We have said that we are not to follow the road on which we trust our own good works to save us. How then should we understand Paul's injunction that the Galatian Christians should not give up doing good? Not trusting our good works for our salvation is quite different from doing good works because we trust Jesus. We are not saved *by* good works but we are saved *for* good works.

This truth is well expressed by Paul when he wrote to the Ephesians. "For it is by grace you have been saved, through faith — and this is not from yourselves, it is the gift of God — not by works, so that no one can boast. For we are God's handiwork, created in Christ Jesus to do good works, which God prepared in advance for us to do" (Ephesians 2:8-10, NIV).

We can understand this further when we remember that our good works as Christians, while they are not to be the basis of our salvation, should be founded on two principles. *Firstly they should arise as a result of our desire and commitment to obey Christ.* We do good because God is good and calls us to be like Him. Jesus explained the law by focusing not only on the things we must not do, but also on the things we must do. The spiritual life is not just about making sure we avoid breaking God's commandments by avoiding any evil that is forbidden by God. We must also remember that sin can be one of commission as well as omission. Stealing is sinful, but not helping a poor beggar when we have an opportunity to do so would also be considered as sinful in the eyes of God.

For Paul, obedience to Christ also involved bringing the gospel to the Gentiles. And what a painful experience that was, when he suffered greatly in the process. But he persevered by the grace of God and brought not only the gospel to the unsaved but also glory to the Saviour.

The second foundation of good works, properly considered within the Christian life, is love. We do good because we learn to love like God. We love because He first loved us. Our relationship with our loving Saviour enables us not only to experience His love firsthand, but also to exhibit that same love in all our relationships. The Lord Jesus summarised the entire Law simply as a call to love God with all our hearts and to love our neighbours as we love ourselves (Matthew 22:37-40).

True Christian obedience is also based on love. Jesus connected love with obedience when He taught His disciples, "If you love me, you will obey what I command," "If anyone loves me, he will obey my teaching" and "Whoever has my commands and obeys them, he is the one who loves me" (John 14:15, 23, 21). Obedience is an essential component of a loving relationship with Jesus. On our own strength we cannot obey God (remember that obedience has outward and inward dimensions; it is both act and motive), but with the power of the indwelling Holy Spirit we are made able to obey God. Out of this obedience will come forth the good works that Paul speaks about.

There is one more thing we must consider to have an adequate understanding of what we are talking about.

Bearing Fruit

Through the power of the Holy Spirit, we will be able to show forth good works because we are good. God does a deep work within us, giving us a new nature and making us Christlike. We actually become good. And our good works will come forth as a result of what is happening within us. This is what Jesus meant when He said, "Likewise every good tree bears good fruit, but a bad tree bears bad fruit" (Matthew 7:17) and also "Each tree is recognized by its own fruit. People do not pick figs from thornbushes, or grapes from briers. A good man brings good things out of the good stored up in his heart, and an evil man brings evil things out of the evil stored up in his heart. For the mouth speaks what the heart is full of" (Luke 6:44-45, NIV).

What is inside will eventually show up. The kind of good works that God wishes to see in the lives of His children arise from who they are or are becoming. The fruit that is shown is neither artificial (as in plastic fruits hung on a tree) nor fruits from elsewhere that are hung on an essentially fruitless tree. The fruitless fig tree, which had nothing but leaves and which was cursed by Jesus for its fruitlessness, could not have been saved by such desperate and deceptive measures. God expects the real good fruit to come from *within* the tree.

The Difference between Producing Fruit and Bearing Fruit

This brings us to the important point that spiritual fruit cannot be manufactured. It has to grow from within. In another of the Lord's teachings, Jesus declared that He is the Vine and we are the branches (John 15:1-17). "No branch can bear fruit by itself; it must remain in the vine" (v. 4). As Andrew Murray helpfully pointed out in the previous century, we are not called to *produce* fruit but to *bear* fruit. To try to produce fruit will bring us into the operation of the flesh even though our intentions may be pious and superficially commendable. It will bring us into the realm of the theology and religion of works.

To bear fruit is to let God do the work. We are to surrender ourselves to His grace and allow His life to flow in and through us. The fruit will then simply follow. This is what Paul meant when He declared, "I no longer live, but Christ lives in me" (Galatians 2:20).

Remaining in Christ

We must not take this to mean that we simply remain passive recipients of God's grace, lifeless branches on which hang God's fruits. Far from it. While producing fruit is God's work, bearing it is ours. Our main work is not to produce spiritual fruit but to remain in Christ. Jesus kept emphasising, "Remain in me." What, then, does the word "remain" mean?

The Greek word from which the English word "remain" is translated is *menō*, which variously means to abide, remain, continue. In the context of John 15, the word could be translated to mean to continue to live in Christ and to be connected with Him in relationship.

How can we continue to remain in Christ? The phrase "in Christ" appears 164 times in the New Testament and is an important way of understanding the Christian life. One way to understand it is to look at ways in which we use similar phrases. When we say that an object in outer space is *in* the solar system, we usually mean that it is a body (like our planet earth) that revolves around the sun. Anything that revolves around the sun and is controlled by its gravity in this way remains within the solar system. An object that is not so ruled by the sun and which does not revolve around the sun is said to be outside the solar system. There are, of course, certain objects that are visitors of the solar system — such as comets and meteors. They visit the system and leave the system. They are not said to be resident in the solar system. To remain in the solar system (the solar kingdom, so to speak), an object must continue under the influence of the sun and revolve around it.

We Remain in Christ by Obeying Him

Likewise, to be in Christ is to come under the command and rule of Christ and to live a Christ-centred life. To remain in Christ is to remain in this relationship of trusting obedience. This has to do with what is expected of us by God. "Remain in me" is a command and we have a choice to obey or not. Jesus does not command us to "produce fruit" or "bear fruit" in John 15, but he does command us to remain in Him. He promises to remain in us if we do so (John 15:4).

The fruitfulness that results from remaining in Christ is what the apostle must have had in mind when he wrote to the Philippians about how he was praying for them. He prayed that they would be "filled with the fruit of righteousness that comes through Jesus Christ" (Philippians 1:11). "The picture is that of an organism that produces fruit, and the one who makes the growth and fruitfulness possible is Jesus Christ."[1]

There are two other realities that Jesus mentions in terms of remaining in Him. He calls us to allow His words to remain in us and for us to remain in His love (John 15:7, 9). This links us with the importance of obedience to Jesus in order to remain in Him. We cannot obey Him if we are not aware of His words or if we fail to take His words seriously or remember them. Even if we know

His words, we cannot truly obey Him (for obedience includes inner motives) without love for Jesus. We have already noted the way Jesus connects love and obedience (John 14:15, 21, 23). Here in John 15, Jesus commands us to remain in His love and then declares that this will be so if we obey His commands (John 15:9-10).

The Role of the Holy Spirit

The words of Christ (thus the Word of God), love for Him, obedience to Him and remaining in Him are all connected in the teaching of Christ. This is where the ministry of the Holy Spirit can be understood. The teaching of the Lord on the vine and the branches is "bookmarked" on either end by His teaching on the Holy Spirit. This is a way of saying that remaining in Christ and abiding in Christ (which then helps us to bear spiritual fruit) is not possible without the continuing ministry of the Holy Spirit.

The Holy Spirit is introduced as "another Counselor" — one who will be in us forever (John 14:16-17). Through the ministry of the Holy Spirit, the Father and the Son will also take residence in us — we will become a home for the Trinity! (John 14:23) The Holy Spirit will make it possible for us to be in a growing and intimate relationship like no other relationship on earth. He will thus enable us to remain in Christ.

The Holy Spirit is also introduced by Jesus as "the Spirit of truth" (John 14:17; 15:26) who will "guide you into all truth" (John 16:13). He will teach the disciples all things and remind them of everything that Jesus had said to them (John 14:26). It is in this way, through the continuing ministry of the Holy Spirit, that we are able to have the words of Jesus remain in us.

We will then be able to obey Jesus — not only because we are reminded by the Spirit of His words, but we will also be enabled to obey those words, since the Spirit is at work to help us will what God wills and to act accordingly (Philippians 2:13). The Spirit who regenerates and enables us to love God will also ensure that our obedience is not as shallow as our outward rituals but as deep as our inner relationship with Christ.

It is in this way that we will be able to bear fruit — as the Spirit works within us. It is in this sense that Paul calls the virtues identified in his list the fruit of the Spirit. Because of the divine initiative and energy behind this process and because it connects us in growing relationship with Jesus, such fruit, according to Him will last (John 15:16). We need the Holy Spirit "to make Jesus real to us" and to help us bear the fruit of the Spirit, the purpose of which is "to reproduce the life and holiness of Jesus within our lives."[2]

Practical Considerations

In conclusion, we can say that spiritual fruit and Christian virtues cannot be produced by self-effort, no matter how pious such self-efforts might be. They are produced when we remain in Christ and the indwelling Spirit of God works within us. The spiritual fruit is produced by God. This is the reason it is called the fruit of the Spirit. Our role is simply to bear this fruit as a result of remaining in Christ and letting Him remain in us. William Law's wise pastoral note that "we cannot lift up a hand, or stir a foot, but by a power that is lent us from God"[3] is something we must always bear in mind.

Does this mean that we have nothing to do or no responsibility for the fruit to emerge and grow in our lives? No, we are in fact called to remain in Christ by *obeying* the commands of Christ because we *love* Him. This is not self-effort, for it is only possible by the empowerment of the indwelling Holy Spirit.

The relationship between submission to the work of God within us and cooperating with God through loving obedience is found in the phrases used by the writer of Hebrews in his description of the example left for us by Jesus — "he was heard because of his *reverent submission*. Although he was a son, he learned *obedience* from what he suffered..." (Hebrews 5:7-8, emphasis added). Christ's reverent submission and obedience need to be found in every believer — if we are to bear the fruit of the very character of Christ. In other words, we are called to *actively submit* to God, actively yielding ourselves to the purposes, presence and power of God.

This will involve self-denial and surrender to God and His ways — resulting in outward and inner obedience. If this is lived as a lifestyle, we will begin to bring forth spiritual fruit and share in the character of Christ. This submissiveness to God is the only way in which we should respond to God's wisdom and love. We do well to ponder the words of the wise Francois Fenelon:

> "We must never hold back anything or resist for a moment this Divine love which searches out self-will in the most secret recesses of the soul. But, on the other hand, it is not a multitude of hard duties, it is not constraint or contention, which advances us in our Christian course. On the contrary, it is to yield our wills without restriction and without choice; to go on cheerfully from day to day as Providence leads us; to seek nothing, to refuse nothing; to find everything in the present moment; and to suffer God, Who does everything, to do His pleasure in and by us, without the slightest resistance."[4]

Fenelon dispels popular notions of submissiveness and makes it look so easy. He is talking about what happens when we make submissiveness to God a habit — it will become a "natural' lifestyle. To observers it will look almost effortless. Most important of all, the one who habitually submits to God is not grumpy or forlorn but full of joy and peace. Fenelon's peaceful picture of submission is built on hidden times of struggle and great effort — with divine grace always providing light on this scene of intense struggle, learned submission and deep serenity.

The word "virtue," Thomas Aquinas said, contains both the ideas of power and habit.[5] This is helpful for our reflection because it tells us that in thinking about the fruit of the Spirit, we have to bring together both grace and cultivation. This connection is something we have noted throughout this chapter. In practice, it means that we must surrender to God's grace through faith and self-denial, while using the means of grace to allow the grace of God to work through us. We have to be faithful in practising spiritual disciplines such as regular Bible reading and meditation, worship and prayer, Christian fellowship and service. As we practise these habits, the Holy Spirit will use them to cultivate His fruit in us.

There are also helpful books and material we can use for personal and group study. An example of a relatively easy book that comes in the form of a hands-on discussion guide is *The Workbook on Virtues and the Fruit of the Spirit.*[6] This book that you are reading is also intended to be another resource to help Christians study, discuss and cultivate the fruit of the Spirit.

In Peter's second epistle, we read that God's "divine power has given us everything we need for a godly life through our knowledge of him who called us by his own glory and goodness. Through these he has given us his very great and precious promises, so that through them you may participate in the divine nature, having escaped the corruption in the world caused by evil desires" (2 Peter 1:3-4). It is clear that God's power and promises are made available to us for our transformation and participation in the divine nature (sharing in Christlikeness).

Does that mean we are to do nothing and simply remain passive? No, for we are called "(f)or this very reason" to "make every effort to add" (2 Peter 1:5, NIV) virtue to virtue so that we may grow in Christlike maturity.[7] The words "make every effort" (also repeated in verse 10) and "add" point to an active discipleship that cooperates with the grace of God and seeks to cultivate the spiritual graces in our life.

This making of every effort has to be seen in the lives of individual Christians, but most importantly it has to be a central feature of church life and ministry. Churches must develop and emphasise spiritual formation programmes and processes that help to build the character of Christ in their members. They have to spend time and effort in thinking through and implementing what Dallas Willard has termed a "curriculum for Christlikeness."[8] We have to be careful that we do not turn this into another flavour-of-the-month popular method. Such processes involve deeper relationships, mentoring, caring, and particular pastoral and skilful attention to matters of the soul. They also take time to develop, in the same way trees grow over the years.

Philip Kenneson showed how important it is to retain the biblical agricultural metaphors — roots, seed, farming and cultivation, harvest — when we think of Christian growth and nurture.

> "(T)hese metaphors and images underscore the importance in the Christian life of both work and grace. All farmers know that there is always more work to be done than there is time to do it; nevertheless, these same farmers also understand that much of what happens to the crops is beyond their control. There is much for the farmer to do, but the farmer cannot make the seed sprout, the sun shine or the rain fall...Grace and effort, gift and works: these must be held together. Unfortunately Christians often either pit these against each other or emphasize one to the exclusion of the other. The wisdom of the farmer reminds us that both are required, in full measure, in order to grow anything worth harvesting. There is always plenty of work to be done, but no one who undertakes that work should do so without realizing that growth in the Spirit is first of all the gift of God."[9]

We will see how this interaction between divine initiative and our cooperation with it works out with reference to the individual characteristics mentioned by Paul as the fruit of the Spirit.

Questions for Reflection

1. What do you think was the basic problem with the way the Pharisees tried to attain holiness? Can you see traces of their approach in contemporary Christianity?

2. What does the Bible say about the flesh or the sinful nature? What are its works? And how can it manifest itself in religious cloths?

3. Divine grace and spiritual effort need not be mutually exclusive. Read Philippians 2:12-13. How does this passage connect trusting God's grace completely and doing something with that grace? Can you share how this actually works out in your life?

4. Compare an unredeemed man who is highly self-disciplined, seeks to be moral and displays some character qualities with a believer who bears the fruit of the Spirit. What similarities and differences would there be? What does it mean to be "in Christ"?

5. What is the connection between "reverent submission" to God (Hebrews 5:7-8) and the bearing of spiritual fruit?

4

LOVE: THE CHIEF FRUIT OF THE SPIRIT

We can now begin to look at the specific list of virtues written by Paul in Galatians. There are nine qualities or virtues in what Paul calls the "fruit of the Spirit" — love, joy, peace, patience, kindness, goodness, faithfulness, gentleness and self-control (Galatians 5:22-23). Each of the following chapters will focus on one of these. Our aim is not only to define and understand them but also to see what the manifestation of these fruits would look like in our lives today, and how we can cooperate with God in their cultivation.

We begin with the first characteristic of the fruit of the Spirit — love. Some commentators have argued that love is *the* characteristic and distinct fruit of the Spirit, and that the other eight character qualities are different aspects of love. Together they give a fuller picture of love as it is described in Scripture and demonstrated in the life of Christ.

There is merit in adopting this perspective as it makes sense in that there is one singular fruit of the Spirit, just as there is one character of Jesus. All the various aspects are interconnected and cannot be dissected too much to be disparate qualities. We saw earlier the dangers of doing so as it leads to a fragmented mechanistic approach that focuses on disparate character traits rather than the whole unified character of Christ which we are called to show forth in our lives.

Our exploration of each of the qualities must therefore be undertaken with this in mind. There are two things that will help us. One is to keep our eyes on Jesus, in whom all these qualities find a fullness and wholeness. Secondly, it helps us to consider love as the core character quality that is related to all the others.

Hence, joy is the energy and colour of love; it is love's joyful song. Peace is the depth of love where we find rest, while patience points to love's maturity and its ability to wait. Kindness is love in action, while goodness is its purity. Faithfulness is the enduring nature of love and its persistence. Gentleness is the beauty of love while self-control is love that is willing to give up self and suffer.

We Learn About Love from the Trinity

The Greek word used here in Paul's list is *agapē* — a word that is used to describe the love that comes from God. Books have been written to define at least four kinds of love based on four Greek words — for example, C. S. Lewis' well-known book, *The Four Loves*, in which he describes different kinds of loves in human life.[1] He considers affection, friendship, *erōs* and charity (divine love). The first three are natural and face the danger of being twisted, and need to be rooted in the fourth.

Erōs is romantic love associated with passion and sexual love. From this word we get the word "erotic." It is personified by the Greek god of love by the same name. This type of love is said to be self-centred as it focuses on the needs and desires of the self. Unlike the other three words, it is not used in the Bible.

Storgē is the family kind of love, found in family relationships.

Phileō is love that is marked by friendship and warm affection.

Agapē is divine love, said to be the highest form of love and characterised by self-giving and sacrificial acts.

While these are differentiated in popular Christian literature, and agape love is seen as the supreme form of love, we must be careful that we do not dissociate them too much so that agape love alone is seen as coming from God, and that the others are natural and human forms of love. God's love covers all the forms of love as His love is the underlying reality in all.

God Himself is described as love (I John 4:8). We need to understand this in the light of what we know of the triune nature of God. Before anything was created, was God able to love someone? If He is love, when God was all alone, how could He have loved? How can the statement "God is love" be applied to Him in that state at that point? Here is where the Christian doctrine of the Trinity is essential in our understanding of God as love.

God is one. As Scripture declares, "The Lord our God, the Lord is one" (Deuteronomy 6:4). At the same time, God is three persons with one nature. That is why we baptise believers in the name (singular) of the three Persons: Father, Son and Holy Spirit (Matthew 28:19). God is one and yet three. This is the mystery that lies at the heart of the Christian doctrine of the Trinity as revealed in Scripture.

Much can be said and much has been written about the Trinity. The doctrine of the Trinity holds together all the different facets of Christian theology and forms the foundation for Christian practice and discipleship. For our discussion, we need to focus only on one aspect — that the Trinity is both a unity and a community. There are eternal relationships within the Trinity that express the love that essentially characterises God. Therefore, we declare that the Son is "eternally begotten of the Father." The Father and the Son are eternally related in a permanent relationship. There never was a time, and never will be a time when this relationship ceases.

We have some light shed on this mystery when Jesus in His high priestly prayer describes His relationship with His Father as "you are in me and I am in you" (John 17:21). How can two persons be in one another? For the Trinity, we have to add the Holy Spirit, who we believe eternally proceeds from the Father and the Son. This "being in one another" has been termed by theologians as *perichoresis* — a Greek word from which we also get the word choreography. This word points to an eternal movement (or dance if you like) that describes how the three Persons of the Trinity are constantly emptying themselves into one another. It shows the Trinity as an eternal stream of self-emptying love. This love was there even before the creation of this world, before time and space were created, before angels and humans were created. It is an eternal quality of the triune

God embedded in the very nature and "structure" of the Godhead.

Dennis Lennon describes this Trinitarian perichoretic dance in this way:

> "The Perichoresis is the dance of pure selflessness, the self-giving of Father to Son, and Son to Father in the Holy Spirit. As the dance moves and turns through the cosmos and through time, the Father approaches the Son with expressions of outpouring in honour of the Son. The Son receives the Father's gifts with joy and gratitude; then, in the dance, he moves towards the Father with gestures of adoring submission to his will. The Spirit of love and glory flows between Father and Son, available to both, ministering to both...The Dance suggests that...we have plunged into and are immersed within the torrent of love and delight, a cascading river of the divine self-outpouring as Father, Son and Spirit give glory to each other without any holding back (Psalm 36: 8,9). In the Cosmic Dance of pure love, 'God only *has* as far as he *gives*, and this giving is of his innermost essence.' Within the Dance, we are bathed in the immensities of God's kindness and generosity as his love flows around and over us. There we glimpse the riches of his self-giving."[2]

The life within the Trinity is characterised by self-giving love and we are invited by this triune God to become His children and taste this life. As we are swept into the immense, deep, and eternal love, we are profoundly astounded and filled with love as we discover that in the depths of this divine ocean of love, we live and thrive rather than die. We find that we have been designed to swim in this ocean and that we have come Home.

This triune God is the Source of all love, and as Christ has put it, is also the very Standard of all Christian love. We are recipients of this love and taste it in Christ. The Father loves us *in the same way* that He loves His eternal Son. Jesus prayed to the Father, "you sent me and have loved them even as you have loved me" (John 17:23). What an astounding truth! God has not held back His love for us.

We are invited to be in the Father and the Son as they are in each other (John 17:21). We are to express the same unity that is in the Trinity — which means that our love for one another must take on the same quality of love that is eternally found within the Trinity (John 17:22). When it comes to the quality of this love, the divine-human barrier is transformed from an impermeable reality to one that is permeable. Jesus prayed, "I in them and you in me" (John 17:23).

In other words, as God's children, according to the unbelievable grace and hospitality of God, we are invited by the triune God to share the life within the Trinity. God has promised as Father, Son and Holy Spirit to move into our hearts and to draw us into His love. The love that eternally flows within the Trinity now overflows missiologically and redemptively, for "God has poured out his love into our hearts by the Holy Spirit, whom he has given us" (Romans 5:5). Now the eternal spring of love has touched us and drawn us into the very life and love of God. This is the mystery and amazing generosity of God's love. It is in this sense that we understand God's call for us to "participate in the divine nature" (2 Peter 1:4).

If we are to understand the reality of love in the Christian life, we must understand the Trinity, for the triune God is the Source of all such love. This Trinitarian love, an inherent and eternal part of God's triune nature, is not only the Source of love but also the Standard of the love that we experience both vertically (divine-human relationship) and horizontally (human relationships). God does not hold back when He loves us. He measures His love in God-sized proportions, for He has loved us in the same way the Persons in the triune Godhead love one another. He also expects us to love one another in the same way — to measure out love in the same extravagant and self-giving way that love has been measured out within the Trinity and from the Trinity to His creation. Therefore, Jesus commands "*As I have* loved you, *so you must* love one another" (John 13:34, emphasis added).

The love that is the fruit of the Spirit and the character of Christ is no less than the Trinitarian love that flows eternally within the Trinity. It is not the cheapened and distorted forms of love that have been diluted beyond recognition in a culture that uses the same word "love" to describe how one feels towards one's spouse, car, pet and ice-cream dessert.

We Learn about Love by Observing Jesus

The love that characterises the fruit of the Spirit was demonstrated by Jesus during His life and ministry on earth. There is much that can be written about this but we will simply make a few points to note this amazing love that Jesus had for His Father as well as for the people of this earth.

How Jesus Loved the Father

Jesus had a profound understanding of His identity and mission. He kept emphasising that He was sent by the Father and had a perfect and intimate relationship with the Father. He loved His Father by being constantly *with* His Father. From eternity, as the Word of God, He was with the Father (John 1:1, emphasis added). "I stand *with* the Father, who sent me" (John 8:16, emphasis added). "The one who sent me is *with* me; he has not left me alone." (John 8:29; 16:32, emphasis added). Jesus had a perfectly intimate relationship with His Father that pointed to the perichoretic love within the Trinity. "Don't you believe that I am in the Father, and that the Father is in me? The words I say to you are not just my own. Rather, it is the Father, living in me, who is doing His work" (John 14:10).

The love of Jesus for His Father was seen not only in His fellowship with the Father but also His faithfulness to the Father. He constantly reiterated the truth that He was sent by the Father (John 3:17; 4:34; 5:30, 36, 38; 6:29, 38, 44; 7:16, 29; 8:16, 18, 26, 29, 8:4ff). Jesus was committed to do the will of the Father and to please Him in every way as the following verses would show:

> "I love the Father...and I do exactly what the Father has commanded me" (John 14:31).

> "I honor my Father" (John 8:49); "I am not seeking glory for myself" (John 8:50).
>
> "I have brought you glory on earth by completing the work you gave me to do" (John 17:4).
>
> "I seek not to please myself but him who sent me" (John 5:30); "I always do what pleases Him" (John 8:29).
>
> "I have come from heaven not to do my will but to do the will of him who sent me" (John 6:38; cf. Luke 22:42).
>
> "My food is to do the will of him who sent me and to finish his work" (John 4:34).

It is clear that Jesus was very focused and single-hearted in His love for the Father. He demonstrated something of that mysterious perichoretic love within the Trinity by giving Himself totally for the pleasure and glory of His Father. He became utterly obedient to His Father, even to the point of death on the cross (Philippians 2:8).

To our modern ears, this would sound problematic for it smacks of immaturity and imprisonment in a relationship of bondage. Part of the problem is the distortions that have taken place in our own human thoughts and experiences. We live in a dog-eat-dog world where the law of the survival of the fittest means that you should not let others take advantage of you. In fact many live by the principle that you should take advantage of others and push yourself forward. In our thoughts too, we have distorted our ideas of maturity by having skewed and delusionary ideas about maturity, independence, freedom and rights.

When we look at the way the Father loved Jesus, we find that He gave Him everything He had — He put all things into the hands of the Son. The Son exhibited the same depth of self-giving love by giving His Father His total allegiance and obedience to the point of giving Himself up with a "not my will but yours be done" attitude. Such self-giving love and total abandonment and obedience are not the work of an immature self or a confused mind, but the actions of perfect maturity. We are, after all, talking about the most perfect of relationships in the universe — that between the Father and the Son.

We may not understand or even be willing to accept the kind of love that we see in Jesus, but if we are to learn about the fruit of the Spirit and the character of Jesus, we must keep looking at Jesus and learn from Him, for He has left us an example to follow.

How Jesus Loved the People

Not only did Jesus love His Father with the Trinitarian love, He also loved the people of this world with that same quality and depth of love. He has loved us in the same way that the Father had loved Him. We can see this in the accounts in the Gospels. He loved His disciples, and ministered to the last, the least and the lost with a compassion that arose from the depths of His being. His love at times came forth as tears, and sometimes as justified and concerned anger. Much of the time, He simply reached out and touched, healed, delivered, and spoke encouraging words.

Ultimately, His love for the world was proven on the painful cross. The Father too loved the world by giving His only Son (John 3:16). Jesus demonstrated that same love by giving Himself on the cross for the redemption of the world. He had told His disciples that "Greater love has no one than this, that he lay down his life for his friends" before calling them His friends (John 15:13-14). Did Jesus die for His friends? Certainly, yes. But we are also told that all of us have sinned and in our minds had become the enemies of God (Colossians 1:21). We all had become ungodly. But Jesus died on the cross for the ungodly (Romans 5:6).

If you were walking along a road and saw a man crossing a road oblivious to a speeding truck heading his way, and realised that he was going to die, how would you feel? Supposing God froze the scene for you and asked you if you were willing to exchange places with that man, would you agree? If the person on the road was a family member we may be willing to go through the "victim-transplant operation." But if it was a friend? Maybe, and that depends. If it was an acquaintance — your neighbour perhaps? Probably not. If it was an enemy? "Most certainly not," most people would respond.

Scripture tells us that Jesus laid down His life for His enemies. He prayed that the Father would forgive those who had put Him on the cross, those who had mocked and tortured Him (Luke 23:34). Jesus lived out what He preached —"Love your enemies and pray for those who persecute you" (Matthew 5:44).

To see the kind of love that characterises the fruit of the Spirit and the character of Christ we have to keep looking at the cross, for there we see an outpouring of the Trinitarian love that did not hold back anything and made the ultimate sacrifice. In our modern age where distorted ideas such as independence, freedom, self-expression and self-actualisation are located in consumerist self-indulgent ways, the cross of Jesus challenges our thinking and shakes our false foundations. It points us to a deep ocean while we play in our little muddy puddles.

We now turn to how this divine love would look like in various aspects of our lives — in our hearts, homes, workplaces, neighbourhoods and society.

How Love Looks Like in the Heart

The Jesus kind of love is something we must aspire to have. We are to "follow the way of love" (1 Corinthians 14:1). The Greek word that is translated "follow" means to pursue eagerly, to seek earnestly to acquire. But this does not mean that we can simply will to be loving like Jesus or that we can psych ourselves up through some psychological technique. Experience would have taught us the futility of all such attempts. The answer lies in abiding or remaining in Christ, to let His Trinitarian love dwell within us through the ministry of the Holy Spirit. When God dwells within, His love would flow into us and from us. This is the secret of what Paul meant when he said, "I no longer live but Christ lives in me" (Galatians 2:20). We remember that Jesus had prayed to the Father, "that the love you have for me may be in them and that I myself may be in them" (John

17:26). The Trinitarian love will be in us (and flow out into our relationships) as Christ dwells within us.

The Case of Peter

We often tend to overestimate our love for God and others. Peter was one such example. He proudly assured Jesus of his love for his master. When Jesus told Peter and the other disciples about His impending death, Peter declared, "Lord I will lay down my life for you" but Jesus asked him, "Will you really lay down your life for me?" and remarked that Peter would in fact let Jesus down by denying Him (John 13:36-38).

Peter was a miserable failure. He did not have the love that he professed. Jesus had shared about the kind of true love that makes a man lay down his life for his friend (John 15:13). But Peter was a poor and unreliable friend — he denied his friendship with Jesus rather than stand with the Man who had loved him so much.

But the love Jesus had for Peter remained. We see that in the way the Risen Jesus reached out to Peter. He sent an angel to the empty tomb to tell the women, "But go, tell his disciples and Peter, He is going ahead of you into Galilee" (Mark 16:7). Note how Peter is singled out, out of special love and consideration. There in Galilee, Jesus met Peter and restored him to ministry and service (John 21).

Three times Jesus asked Peter, "Do you love me?" with different variations. Perhaps the fire used to cook breakfast and the question asked three times would have brought Peter to the point of his earlier failure — what a painfully embarrassing memory (Luke 22:54-62). He now had a chance to redeem the situation. The first time, Jesus asked Peter, "do you truly love me more than these", He used the wonderful word *agapē*, and his phrase "more than these" could have referred to the other disciples against whom Peter had proudly compared himself by saying "Even if all fall away I will not" (Mark 14:29). Or the phrase could have referred to the fish that Peter had managed to catch after following the instructions of Jesus — which if true, would have pointed to the need for Peter to choose between his profession to which he had returned and His Lord whom He must now follow to the end.

The quality of love in Jesus' question was indeed high — as rich as the self-giving Trinitarian kind, reminiscent of Peter's earlier professions of love for Jesus. Imagine Jesus extending both His hands with His inward-facing palms the furthest distance from each other (indicating the extent of Peter's love) when asking the question. Peter must have been embarrassed by His dismal failure, and in his reply used the word *phileō* when answering the question posed by Jesus.

The second time Jesus asked the question, He dropped the phrase "more than these" but retained the word *agapē*. It was as if Jesus had brought His hands closer together when asking Peter how much he loved Jesus. Peter's answer continued to be in the region of *phileō* love. Finally Jesus dropped the superlatives and simply asked whether Peter loved Him. This time He used the *phileō* word, as if coming down to where Peter really was. Peter was hurt as he came to terms with the reality of his love but declared humbly his feeble and limited love for Jesus. The Lord then told Peter how he must lay down his life for Jesus further down the way — and surely must have reminded Peter of their earlier conversation of how a true friend must be willing to lay down his life for his friend.

God Empowered Love

At the Pentecost experience in Acts 2, Peter and the other disciples were filled with the Holy Spirit and Peter was able to experience a new surge of supernatural power, as the indwelling power of the Holy Spirit brought him into the realm of Trinitarian love. He lived his life loving Jesus and the people to whom Jesus sent him. Eventually as Jesus had predicted, Peter was crucified in Rome, and as tradition has it, he requested to be crucified upside down, counting himself unworthy to be crucified in exactly the same manner as his Lord.

Love produced by the indwelling Spirit trusts God and shows that trust through a life of obedience. It is prepared to go beyond the self and is willing to lay down its life for a friend, or even an enemy. Above all, it brings the self to the altar in obedience to and love for God.

This love will grow within us when we keep our eyes on the cross of Jesus and continue to discover more deeply what God has done for us. Charles Wesley was converted when he realised how personal was the verse "I live by faith in the Son of God, who loved *me* and gave himself for *me*" (Galatians 2:20, emphasis added). To him, the word "me" in that verse became a personal experience as he recognised God's love for him on the cross. A continuing experience like this will help and enable us to live in Christ and to let Him live His life in us as the preceding verse shows: "I no longer live but Christ lives in me" (Galatians 2:20).

Meditating on the word of God, fixing our eyes on the cross, engaging in prayer that experiences the loving presence of God — such disciplines would help develop gratitude to God in our hearts. It is with this gratitude that our love for God would grow and find expression daily in acts of love for God and in His name for others.

How Love Looks Like at Home

Many would consider it quite natural to love one's family members. We even use the term "loved ones" when referring to them. The love of a mother who nurses her sick child throughout the night, the love of a father who would instinctively protect his daughter from attackers, the dead mother in whose shielding arms a baby is found alive in a tragic fire — all these are reported in newspapers from time to time and strengthen our appreciation of familial love.

Contemporary Challenges

However we also increasingly read about gross examples of abuse in the family — of mothers murdering their children or fathers molesting their daughters, or children beating or neglecting their aging parents. Child and elder abuse, spousal violence, family breakups all point to a decline in love — even in the family. This may be attributed to various factors such as growing individualism, self-centredness and self-indulgence, consumerist behaviour and a general loss of values and virtues.

It is in this context that a Christian must make a difference at home. The Spirit's fruit of love can make a significant difference in the way relationships in the family are experienced. Jack and Judith Balswick have shown the kind of transformation that can be effected by such divine power in relationships.[3] Instead of hurting one another, family members will empower and minister to one another. Instead of hiding from one another in isolation, there will be communication, intimacy and healthy interaction. Instead of blaming one another, they will, in grace, forgive, encourage and affirm one another. The family will increasingly be seen as a place where persons are loved and will love in covenantal relationships.

Of course, there will be times when the fallen human nature will cause disappointment, misunderstanding and frustration. But where else would forgiveness need to be practised than in the family? In the parable of the prodigal son, the father's forgiving love makes him hope for the best and wait for his ungrateful and prodigal son to return. And when he does, after repenting of his sin, the father lavishes his love on the son with generosity and grace. The elder son resents this and is unable to forgive his lost and found brother. Such dynamics are played out again and again in family life.

Practising Love at Home

The indwelling Spirit and the character of Christ can make a profound difference in family life. Introducing divine love in familial relationships strengthens and enriches them. This is achieved through the power of the Holy Spirit, a reality that is necessary often in counselling situations involving families. Familial relationships can also be enhanced through certain spiritual disciplines and habits that one can build in one's life.

For instance, family members must be seen in the light of God's perspective. They are not our possessions to be used and enjoyed, but God's gifts to us. In Tamil, the word for parents (*petroar*) is a wonderful word that simply means "those who receive" — they receive their children from God, a truth that is emphasised in the Bible. "Sons (and daughters) are a heritage from the Lord, children a reward from him" (Psalm 127:3). This truth and the attitude it produces introduce the dimension of stewardship in our closest relationships. We are entrusted by God with our loved ones. Our responsibility is founded on the principle of love — love for God who gave us our family members to look after, and love for our family members who are to be loved rather than be merely used for our purposes or ambitions. With this attitude we will value our family members as persons and for who they are. It means that we will give them a listening ear, we will give them their space, and practise hospitality at home.

This is expounded further by Paul in his description of the husband-wife relationship (Ephesians 5:22-33). Husbands are to love their wives (and Christ is the example used, in the way He loves the church, His bride). Wives, on their part, must submit and respect their husbands — as to the Lord, and because of their love for God and their husbands. Likewise, fathers are not to exasperate their children but rather, by implication, encourage their children, even as their children are expected to show their love for their parents by obeying them (Ephesians 6:1-4).

It is interesting and helpful to note that Paul describes such family relationships after his imperative "be filled with the Spirit" (Ephesians 5:18). A consequence of being filled with the Spirit is that we will bear the fruit of the Spirit and reflect the love of Christ in our relationships. This will show up in a family life that builds, nurtures, empowers, and blesses.

We can pray for family members regularly, bringing each into the light and grace of God as we pray for them. Such praying will help us to love them and reflect on their real needs and how we can meet them. We can find time for family members, building such priorities in our schedules and diaries. We must seek to be present in their lives when we are needed. Like Jesus, we can express such love in the form of obedience — for instance, when He obeyed his parents at home even though He realised that they did not understand His pronouncements at the temple (Luke 2:50-51). Paul does say that we are to "submit to one another out of reverence for Christ" (Ephesians 5:21). Such mutual submission is not possible without having the fruit of the Spirit.

How Love Looks Like at the Workplace

Divine love at the workplace would take the shape of justice and compassion, integrity and kindness. Elsewhere I have written on the importance of the conscience at the workplace.[4] Such a functioning conscience would be shaped by the Word of God and the Spirit that also produces the fruit of love. Love would be one of the elements that would make the conscience work properly.

This would mean that an employer would treat his employees fairly and as fellow human beings by providing for them what is fair and right (Colossians 4:1). Besides writing to the Colossians while he was in prison in Rome, Paul also wrote to his friend Philemon. Philemon had a slave by the name of Onesimus who had run away from his master. Paul writes to Philemon urging him to forgive and accept Onesimus. He makes his appeal "on the basis of love" (Philemon 1:9), using terms of endearment when speaking of Onesimus ("who became my son while I was in chains"; "my very heart"). He requests Philemon to re-employ Onesimus and to accept him as a brother and partner, welcoming him as he would welcome his friend Paul himself. The atmosphere of the entire letter is fragranced by divine love.

Not only should such consideration be given to one's subordinates at the workplace, but the same needs to be seen in working relationships with colleagues. One must desist from backbiting or engaging in unhealthy competitiveness at the workplace. One's attitude to one's superiors should also display similar attitudes. Respect and wholehearted honest service are the marks of one who is filled with the Holy Spirit (Ephesians 6:5-8). The underlying motive is love for God (and his laws and ways) and loving consideration of those we work for, or work with.

Recently an older Christian shared with me how he nearly ended up in the uniformed services. But he had a problem — he realised that as he was required to carry a gun, he would have great difficulty using it to shoot someone else. His logic went this way: if that person dies and he does not know the Lord, his end would be tragic; it would be better in such an encounter that it was me who died rather than him, as he would be given an opportunity to know the Lord and have his eternal destiny changed. This gentleman ended up in a different occupation.

Not every Christian may share his views, but his point is interesting. How do we look at those around us? How do we look at our colleagues, especially those who have yet to come to know Christ? If we truly love them would we not be concerned about their eternal salvation? Such concern would be shown in the way we listen to, care for and share with them. Our conversations with colleagues will, from time to time, take on a more meaningful and deeper texture. We will get to know them not just as digits but as human beings — with their own aspirations, problems and struggles. We will pray for them.

How Love Looks Like in the Church

The church is the new society that God has established to reflect the dynamic and values of the Kingdom of God according to God's promises in the new covenant. At the heart of the church is being the body of Christ (1 Corinthians 12) and the temple of the Holy Spirit (1 Corinthians 3:16). The fruit of such life is love. Jesus commanded His disciples, "A new commandment I give to you: Love one another. As I have loved you, so you must love one another. By this all men will know that you are my disciples, if you love one another" (John 13:34-35, NIV).

This love that Jesus talks about is the love that is to be found in the relationships between believers in the church. While this dynamic is extended to include others outside the church in the injunction, this particular command "Love your neighbours" is for the church family. It is a reflection of familial relationships; hence believers are brothers and sisters to each other. In fact, it goes even deeper than natural familial relationships; it is supernatural both in its source and standard. Such love is possible only in Spirit-filled people and Spirit-filled churches, for it is indeed the fruit of the Spirit. It is a love the standards and quality of which lie in the way Jesus has loved us and continues to love us — "As I have loved you..."

This love within the church is expressed in numerous ways in the phrase "one another" used in the New Testament. Thus we are to love one another in numerous ways. A few of these can be listed below:

Mark 9:50	"...be at peace with one another."
John 13:14	"...you also should wash one another's feet."
John 13:34	"As I have loved you, so must you love one another."
Romans 12:10	"Be devoted to one another in brotherly love..."
Romans 14:13	"Therefore let us stop passing judgment on one another..."
Romans 14:19	"Make every effort to do what leads to peace and to mutual edification."
Romans 16:16	"Greet one another..."
1 Corinthians 11:33	"...wait for each other."
Galatians 5:13	"...serve one another."
Galatians 6:2	"Carry each other's burdens..."
Ephesians 4:2	"[Show] tolerance for one another in love."
Ephesians 4:32	"Be kind to one another..."
Ephesians 5:21	"Submit to one another out of reverence for Christ."
Philippians 2:3	"Consider others better than yourselves."
Colossians 3:13	"Bear with each other and forgive."
Colossians 3:16	"Teach and admonish one another..."
1 Thessalonians 5:11	"Therefore encourage one another and build up each other..."
1 Thessalonians 5:13b	"Live in peace with each other."

1 Thessalonians 5:15	"...always try to be kind to each other..."
Hebrews 10:24	"Spur one another on toward love and good deeds..."
James 5:9	"Don't grumble against each other..."
James 5:16	"Therefore, confess your sins to each other, and pray for each other..."
1 Peter 4:9	"Offer hospitality to one another without grumbling."

The logic in the teachings of Jesus is that if we, who have the same Father, Lord and Spirit, cannot love one another in church, how can we love others outside the church? The living evidence that we belong to God and have been sent by Him is the profound divine love in the way we relate to one another in church. There are many people who are not convinced that it is necessary for them to turn to Christ (and join the church) when they see the lack of love — or even the ugly fights that occur in churches from time to time. Paul picks up the same point to urge his readers not to give up doing good to all people, "especially to those who belong to the family of believers" (Galatians 6:10).

Love Rejects Sinful Social Prejudices

Such supernatural divine love will characterise how the church welcomes its family members. In the church, false and sinful hierarchies that marginalise groups of people based on gender, social class and ethnicity are to be discarded. The social sins of the world must end at the door of the church when believers gather to worship God, for "there is neither Jew nor Gentile, neither slave nor free, nor is there male and female, for you are all one in Christ Jesus" (Galatians 3:28, NIV).

Alas, how strongly and stubbornly sinful social prejudices are lodged in us such that even in church, the principles of the world are often visible. This demonstrates the lack of the fruit of the Spirit. The early church also struggled with such problems, as the apostle James points out. "My brothers, as believers in our glorious Lord

Jesus Christ, don't show favoritism. Suppose a man comes into your meeting wearing a gold ring and fine clothes, and a poor man in shabby clothes also comes in. If you show special attention to the man wearing fine clothes and say, 'Here's a good seat for you,' but say to the poor man, 'You stand there' or 'Sit on the floor by my feet,' have you not discriminated among yourselves and become judges with evil thoughts?" (James 2:1-4). Our seating arrangements and leadership appointments in church must not be based on principles of worldly success or skills.

Reaching Out to the Needy

Divine love goes particularly to the poor and needy. It is neither blind nor unresponsive to their needs. This is to be seen in the church too. In the early church, they showed practical love by doing something quite radical. "All the believers were one in heart and mind. No one claimed that any of his possessions was his own, but they shared everything they had...*There were no needy persons among them*" (Acts 4:32, 34, emphasis added). Two things must be noted here. First, the description of the church here followed the observation that "they were all filled with the Holy Spirit" after they prayed together as a church (Acts 4:31). The spiritual dynamic is clear. The filling of the Holy Spirit produces a supernatural love that defies the sinful and selfish patterns of our world.

Second, rarely (or perhaps never) since that early snapshot of the church has there been a similar picture of a church filled with such love for one another so that in reality there was no needy person in the congregation. How many congregations do we know that can confidently and honestly say that? Probably none.

Exercising the Gifts of the Spirit

Divine love in church is seen not only in the way we reject social injustices and disparities, and reach out to needy persons, but also in the way we exercise the Spirit's gifts. The whole tenor of Paul's response to the rather chaotic exercise of spiritual gifts in the Corinthian church was to show how important love was in the exercise of gifts. Otherwise, it is simply noise and spectacle, with no benefit to anyone. It would simply be a show filled with pride, disunity and unhealthy competitiveness. Paul wrote those famous words:

> "If I speak in the tongues of men and of angels, but have not love, I am only a resounding gong or a clanging cymbal. If I have the gift of prophecy and can fathom all mysteries and all knowledge, and if I have a faith that can move mountains, but have not love, I am nothing. If I give all I possess to the poor and surrender my body to the flames, but have not love, I gain nothing" (1 Corinthians 13:1-3).

Only if love infuses all that we say and do in church will our worship be orderly and reflective of the beauty and majesty of God, our ministries truly edifying, and our witness truly convincing to a watching world. Observers will have a better reason to come to the conclusion, "God is really among you!" (1 Corinthians 14:25).

Otherwise our programmes and institutions will become more important than the people in them. Success will be our obsession rather than faithfulness. We will end up using people rather than loving them. We could end up as legalists or smart entrepreneurs in church. But we need to recognise that God has gathered us to be His flock where we will be challenged to be equipped with all good gifts (if we wait upon God to receive from Him), and to give constant regard to each other and love one another the way God loves us.

How Love Looks Like in the Neighbourhood and Wider Society

The Bible is rich with teaching on the kind of society that God had in mind when He established the nation of Israel. A few examples would suffice here. God is concerned about the poor and needy (especially widows and orphans, and sometimes foreigners) and expects His people to have the same attitude (Deuteronomy 10:18; Exodus 22:21-22). When harvesting, God expected farmers in the promised land to avoid harvesting the land clean but to leave behind some grains for the poor (Leviticus 23:22). Those who were in debt were not to be burdened with stifling interest (Exodus 22:25) and were to be periodically released from their debts (Deuteronomy 15:1-11). A man who gives up his cloak as surety for a loan must be returned that cloak before the cold night falls so that he would not suffer or die in the cold (Exodus 22:26-27). The general principle was to avoid taking advantage of others. "Do not take advantage of each other, but fear your God" (Leviticus 25:17).

Unfortunately, this ideal was hardly seen in Israel as the people fell into idolatry and sin. The prophet Ezekiel was shown the real condition of Israel — the leaders (together with their people) were "each at the shrine of his own idol" in the darkness (Ezekiel 8:12). In reality, it is usually the case that one's greatest idol is oneself, for self-centredness and pride are the biggest problems in the human heart. A selfish, self-driven and self-worshipping society would create all kinds of social aberrations and problems. And that was the situation in Israel as eloquently spelled out by the messages of the ancient biblical prophets. People were cheating and killing and abusing one another.

Years later, Paul spelt out the kind of pagan society he lived in: "They have become filled with every kind of wickedness, evil, greed and depravity. They are full of envy, murder, strife, deceit and malice. They are gossips, slanderers, God-haters, insolent, arrogant and boastful; they invent ways of doing evil; they disobey their parents; they have no understanding, no fidelity, no love, no mercy" (Romans 1:29-31, NIV). Paul described a society with little evidence of love. Such social realities have not changed much. It may even have worsened in our world today where self-centredness and a utilitarian attitude towards all are celebrated as the characteristics of winners and necessary for personal success. As some say, it is a dog-eat-dog world — a Darwinian jungle.

It was in this kind of world that Paul saw the need to enter with God's truth, hope and love. He was called by God to proclaim the Good News and to live out the Good News in a fallen world. Paul left behind a better world, at least in places where he touched people's lives. His concern for people without salvation, and his concerns for those in need reflected the same attitude and actions of Jesus. The Lord had ministered to people, challenging injustices in his own special way, healing people, bringing about reconciliation, and guiding those who were lost. He had time for those who were marginalised, neglected, forgotten or ignored.

At the judgment, Jesus said that we will be judged by how we showed love or failed to show God's love in society. He would say to those who pleased him, "For I was hungry and you gave me something to eat, I was thirsty and you gave me something to drink, I was a stranger and you invited me in, I needed clothes and you clothed me, I was sick and you looked after me, I was in prison and you came to visit me" (Matthew 25:35-36).

How then can we show God's love as we go about our daily business and routines? Somerset Ward notes that it is the small, daily things we do that significantly shape our character:

> "The necessary materials for the building up of a saint are in every life; they need only to be used...It is not necessary to be hung upon a cross in order to be crucified; an idle slander accepted meekly will do instead. It is not necessary to kiss a leper to secure self-discipline; a genuine effort to be kind and companionable to a person we dislike intensely will do as well. It is not necessary to face martyrdom before a heathen judge to secure a severe test, for the humble acceptance of a sudden insult or the true and instant forgiveness of a wrong will serve as well."[5]

If we have something of the character of Jesus, we would each day consider how we can express God's love and salvation to those we meet every day — as we drive on the road, as the old man working in the petrol station pumps petrol into our cars, as we do our shopping, as we travel, as we pass by poor people.

Questions for Reflection

1. Why is it important to reflect on the Trinity in order to understand God's love? Read the section in the chapter on the divine *perichoresis*. What new lessons have you learned about God's love that He has shared with us?

2. Review the verses mentioned in the chapter concerning how Jesus loved the Father. How do they challenge you? Why are we expected to love God the same way Jesus loved the Father?

3. Why is it difficult to love our enemies? What did Jesus say and show about how to love enemies?

4. Why do we tend to ignore love in the daily course of our lives? What modern factors tend to make us less loving? Discuss what you have discovered on love in the various spheres of life — home, church, workplace, society. What specific steps can you take in order to reflect more effectively and sincerely the love of God?

5

JOY: WHEN LOVE SINGS

The Christian life is one filled with joy — a truth that is often misunderstood because of confusion regarding the basis and reality of joy.

Thomas Aquinas, in his *Summa Theologica*, wrote on the connections and differences between pleasure, happiness and joy.[1] It is important to know the differences if we are to live lives that are faithful to God. The American Christian philosopher Peter Kreeft summarises it in this way: "Joy is more than happiness, just as happiness is more than pleasure. Pleasure is in the body. Happiness is in the mind and feelings. Joy is deep in the heart, the spirit, the center of the self."[2]

Pleasure, Happiness and Joy

Pleasure has to do with enjoyable experiences, often bodily mediated. It is what you get when you enjoy something physically or mentally, like when you enjoy a good cup of coffee or a piece of music. There is nothing wrong with these things since God has created us to enjoy the good things in life, but they are neither the basis of joy, nor do they provide the ultimate meaning of life. This is because they are self-referenced. One enjoys it for oneself.

Happiness has to do with pleasant circumstances coming together to give you a sense of wellbeing. The focus is on circumstances. When your doctor gives you a clean bill of health or when you are going for a nice holiday, you feel happy. On the other hand, when you receive bad news or when life's circumstances are not pleasant, you feel unhappy and sad. Happiness, too, does not provide the ultimate meaning for life.

It is interesting that discussions are taking place on how one can measure the wellbeing of a country. Should we only look at the GDP — the level of financial wealth of a country — to measure how well it is doing? Some argue that we should measure the "happiness index" of the people of a country. This has to do with things that cannot be bought with money — things that have to do more with contentment with one's circumstances. The consumer-driven and pleasure-directed activities of modern economic life tend to focus on pleasure — just think of the latest gadgets, spas, movies, restaurants, and so on. There are people who have questioned such a relentless pursuit of personal wellbeing that is restricted to fleeting pleasures bought by growing wealth. So let's measure the happiness index of societies, they say.

This brings us to reflect on joy. Joy does not depend on pleasure or happy circumstances. It primarily depends on living healthy and growing relationships. This is why, even in pain one can have joy, or even when the circumstances are not necessarily going well, one can still rejoice. We must remember that at the heart of the Christian faith (and all of human life) is relationships — our vertical relationship with God and our horizontal relationships with others. We are created for relationships by the God who is defined by eternal relationships within the Godhead.

This is also why love and joy are deeply connected. Joy is present where love is present, and likewise is absent when love is absent. In pleasure the focus is on pleasant sensations; in happiness, the focus is on pleasant circumstances. In joy the focus is on the love that characterises restored and healthy (and ultimately pleasant) relationships.

It is for this reason that the Bible's command that we should be "joyful always" and the emphasis that this is the will of God (1 Thessalonians 5:16) is not merely a nice slogan that is impractical and idealistic. It is a real possibility available to all Christians based on our relationship with our Lord Jesus. It is He who said that no one can snatch us from His hands and the Father's hands (John 10:28-29). God has promised that He would never leave us nor forsake us (Hebrews 13:5). Because we are commanded to remain in constant communion with Christ, it makes sense that we should also have a command to always be joyful. This joy wells up from a heart that is connected with Jesus, and it is a by-product of the love that is given by the Holy Spirit as a gift to us. Let us explore this further in terms of our relationship with God and with others.

Jesus and Joy

The Greek word that is translated as "joy" in Galatians 6 is *chara*. It is also associated with the word *charis*, meaning grace, suggesting connections between grace and joy. Joy is a gift of God's grace and is freely given to us. At the birth of Jesus, the angels announced to the frightened shepherds, "I bring you good news of great joy that will be for all the people" (Luke 2:10). Our joy has to do with Jesus, God's wonderful and indescribable gift to us.

Jesus was the perfect expression of divine joy. We are used to calling Him the man of sorrows, following the prophecy regarding Him in Isaiah 53:3 where the Servant of the Lord is described. That points to His suffering and passion, but not to His personality — certainly He was not depressed or dour. In fact, there was often a sense of humour in the way Jesus told stories or spoke to people. Elton Trueblood wrote a book *The Humour of Christ* to show that behind many sayings of Jesus was wit and humour and often a sense of amused irony.[3] This can also be noted in several of the parables Jesus told.

Jesus rejoiced in His ability to reach out to sinful people who were shunned by the religious Pharisees, and His joy in seeing them repent and turn to God resulted in accusations that He was socialising with publicans and sinners and that He was a "glutton and a drunkard, a friend of tax collectors and 'sinners'" (Luke 7:34). The self-righteous Pharisees and teachers of the law observed with distaste and envy as the publicans and sinners gathered around Jesus, and criticised Him, "This man welcomes sinners and eats with them" (Luke 15:2). They did not know anything about the joy of salvation, which Jesus then went about to discuss using three parables on salvation.

Joy in our Relationship with God

True joy is found in our relationship with God. This is the reason why Scripture constantly speaks about the joy of salvation. We are all alienated from God because the burden and presence of our sins are both offensive to God. We have all been driven (as the first Adam was) from God's delightful Garden where God used to commune with man. Like the prodigal son, we have become homeless and lonely. But man has designed all kinds of ways to hide and deny the fact that he is alienated from God and missing something very significant in his life. Some people do this by denying that God exists or claiming that even if He does, He is irrelevant. Others do so by filling their life with fleeting pleasures and happiness — their achievements, wealth, power, smartness and strength. But the gnawing emptiness within cannot be filled by anything from this world because we have been designed to be related to God in a loving relationship.

God sent His Son to solve the problems of the human race, so that anyone who believes in Jesus and receives Him as Lord and Saviour will have the joy of becoming a child of God (John 1:12). Hence, when a sinner repents from his sin and reconnects with God, there is much joy — in God's heart as well as in the sinner's heart.

Jesus told many parables to depict this joy. Luke 15 contains three of them: the lost sheep, the lost coin and the lost son — all told in response to the criticism of the religious leaders that He was consorting with sinners. The connecting theme in these stories is the joy that overflows when what was lost is found.

> "I tell you that in the same way there will be more rejoicing in heaven over one sinner who repents than over ninety-nine righteous persons who do not need to repent" (Luke 15:7).

> "In the same way, I tell you, there is rejoicing in the presence of the angels of God over one sinner who repents" (Luke 15:10).

> "Let's have a feast and celebrate. For this son of mine was dead and is alive again; he was lost and is found. So they began to celebrate" (Luke 15:23-24).

Because joy is based on relationship, when we turn to God in repentance and experience a restored relationship with God, we experience the joy that flows from that relationship. For many, the first time this relationship is experienced in a new way, it is indeed a very special experience. It has been variously described as the lifting of an immense burden, the inflowing of God's presence, and the shining of God's light within. It has been marked with overflowing tears and a bursting forth with new song. In the case of John Wesley, who lived in the 18th century, it was his "strangely-warmed" heart that marked the experience. He wrote in his journal of his experience on 24 May 1738:

> "In the evening I went very unwillingly to a society in Aldersgate Street, where one was reading Luther's preface to the Epistle to the Romans. About a quarter before nine, while he was describing the change which God works in the heart through faith in Christ, *I felt my heart strangely warmed.* I felt I did trust in Christ, Christ alone, for salvation; and an assurance was given me that He had taken away my sins, even mine, and saved me from the law of sin and death"[4] (emphasis added).

Wesley's brother, Charles, also had a similar experience on 21 May 1738 on Whit Sunday (Pentecost) and wrote a famous hymn (his first) two days later to mark the occasion. The first two stanzas of the song, "Where Shall My Wandering Soul Begin" are:

"Where shall my wondering soul begin?
How shall I all to heaven aspire?
A slave redeemed from death and sin,
A brand plucked from eternal fire,
How shall I equal triumphs raise,
Or sing my great Deliverer's praise?

O how shall I the goodness tell,
Father, which Thou to me hast showed?
That I, a child of wrath and hell,
I should be called a child of God,
Should know, should feel, my sins forgiven,
Blest with this antepast of heaven!"[5]

Both John's prose and Charles' poetry speak of the joy of restored relationship with God and the gift of this relationship received through the atoning work of Jesus Christ and the assuring testimony of the Holy Spirit. The joy that is part and parcel of this relationship with God is ours to keep forever since we have been called to be in this relationship forever.

Joy in His Presence

There is joy in God's presence like nowhere else. David, as royal psalmist of Israel, sang often of the joy that is found in God's great and wonderful presence. One such example is Psalm 21, where David sang of his joy in witnessing the presence of God in the many victories that he experienced as king. He comes to the heart of the matter when, in referring to the king (himself), he writes: "Surely you have granted him eternal blessings and made him glad with *the joy of your presence*" (v 6, emphasis added). In the following verse, David speaks about his relationship with God expressed in the words, "For the king trusts in the Lord; through the unfailing love of the Most High he will not be shaken" (v 7).

We cannot fail to notice the unfailing love of God that David experienced and his response of trusting God. The words "love" and "trusts" speak volumes of the quality of God's relationship with David. Hence, there was much joy in David's heart in God's presence. There are some things we must note about this joy in God's presence and some habits we must develop to maintain it, in cooperation with God's grace.

Confess Sin

Our relationship with God, restored and renewed, gives us unprecedented joy. However, Christians do not always keep this joy. They can lose it along the way. This happens when sin gets in the way, and when that happens it is important that we confess our sins before God and reject them. Only then can the joy return. David, who sinned terribly against God and denied his sin for some time, was shattered when his sin was pointed out to him. He wrote and pleaded with God in heartfelt repentance, "Restore to me the joy of your salvation and grant me a willing spirit to sustain me" (Psalm 51:12). David missed the joy he had with God because of his present sin, and having confessed his sin, wished sincerely that sin would not come in the way of his relationship with God. Hoping for no more disruptions, he prayed to God for a "willing spirit" that would readily do God's will and depart from all evil ways.

Unconfessed sins (both the committed and omitted varieties) take away the joy of salvation. That is the reason why we have (and unfortunately, because they have been discontinued or forgotten in many churches today, used to have) the prayer of confession at the beginning of the liturgy of worship. We seek forgiveness of sins in God's presence, realising that the work of salvation (of perfecting us in holy love) is yet to be completed. When we receive forgiveness, our joy is restored; then we can truly sing for joy (not just because the tune or beat is nice but) because we have been forgiven by our merciful God in response to our heartfelt confession of our present sins and sinful ways. It is strange that modern Christians can conceive of going directly into singing without any thought to their ongoing sins or the need to confess them and to receive God's ongoing forgiveness. Such presumptuousness on our part will not bring us truly into God's holy presence or into the real joy of our salvation.

Worship God

Scripture connects worship with joy. If we remember that joy is based on relationships, we can understand why. We come into the presence of God not to perform empty rituals or to rouse ourselves to engage in some great projects or even to hear some informative lectures. We come into God's presence to remember who He is and what He has done for us (Psalm 107:22), to celebrate His presence in our lives, to thank Him for all He is and does and to express our love for Him. From the beginning till the end, the worship service should be grounded in our relationship with God, and therefore should be characterised by the joy that comes from it.

Joy is expressed by people in different ways according to their temperament and age. We should not spend time to argue about which way is best. What is important is that the joy must be real, expressed at the foot of the cross of Jesus, maintained by true repentance, and connected with our relationship with God who is holy and merciful. Being forgiven, we can turn to joyful worship as we tell God, "you removed my sackcloth and clothed me with joy" (Psalm 30:11).

God will become the very reason of our joy as we behold His glory and compassion. The whole world and all its possessions cannot buy the joy of knowing this faithful and loving God. "Then I will go to the altar of God, *to God*, my joy and my delight" (Psalm 43:4, 13, emphasis added). The psalmist in worship goes to the altar, but realises that in doing so he is indeed going to God. The focus ultimately is not the furniture and furnishings in church but the God we profess to worship. When our attention is truly drawn to Him, we will experience anew the joy of salvation.

We will then be able to sing to God joyfully (Psalm 66:1) and in our joy invite all nature to sing along with us (Psalm 96:11-13) even as, in our jubilation, we hear the "music of the spheres" (as we sing in the wonderful hymn "This is My Father's World").

Our worship in church must continue to be reflected in our personal daily lives. This means that we must regularly confess our sins before God so that nothing comes between us and God to take away the joy of salvation. J. I. Packer in his book *Rediscovering Holiness* writes about the wonderful testimony of John Bradford (1510-1555), an English Puritan who was burned at the stake at the age of 45.[6] What characterised Bradford's life was a lifetime and lifestyle of repentance. He saw the continuous need for personal repentance (in the light of the fear and love of God) and thus found heights of holiness and joy rarely experienced. Writing from profound experience, he advises:

> "Only in thy prayer away with the purpose of sinning, for he that prayeth with a purpose to continue in any sin cannot be heard...away therefore with the spots of purposing to continue in sin. Bid adieu, when thou goest to prayer, bid adieu, I say, and farewell to thy covetousness, to thy uncleanness, swearing, lying, malice, drunkenness, gluttony, idleness, pride, envy, garrulity, slothfulness, negligence, &c. If thou feelest thy wilful and perverse will unwilling thereunto, out of hand complain it to the Lord, and for His Christ's sake pray Him to reform thy wicked will...that by Christ it should be to His glory to give 'to men a good will,' to consent to His will, and therein to delight night and day. The which is that happiness which David singeth of in his first psalm: therefore more earnestly crave it, and cease not till thou get it..."[7]

Such an attitude towards God and to our sins would keep the relationship with God fresh and healthy, and help to maintain the unspeakable joy that comes from that relationship.

Not only can we make confession and repentance a spiritual habit, we can also make the worship of God an important aspect of our daily routines. Keeping a regular devotional time (preferably early in the morning) when we can worship God and pray to Him, thus enjoying the joy found in His presence, is an essential part of the formation of spiritual habits. There are many aids available to help us, such as daily Bible readings, prayer books, hymnals and devotional literature. The key point is to develop a habit of worshipping God. This we can carry into our other activities; whenever we have an opportunity we can sing a song quietly in our hearts, praise and thank God for something, or bring a concern or person to Him in prayer. Such vitality in our relationship with God will keep the joy that is a treasure in the Christian life.

We would remember the promise of Jesus to His troubled disciples when they heard about His impending death. "So with you: Now is your time of grief, but I will see you again and you will rejoice, and no one will take away your joy" (John 16:22). Jesus, though taken away from them to die on the cross, will return to them and be reunited with them in a new way. When the Spirit comes, He will be reunited with them forever. Their joy will find a new reality and cannot be taken away, neither by Caesar nor by circumstances. Jesus has promised this joy of being forever united with Him. We can celebrate it every day of our lives.

Read and Obey God's Word

In that great psalm on the Word of God, the psalmist declares to God, "Your statutes are my heritage forever; they are the joy of my heart" (Psalm 119:111). The Word of God is connected with the joy of the Christian life. That is because the Word of God is the normal and appointed means by which we hear the living voice of God. The Bible connects our minds with the mind of God. When we read it our hearts are connected with God's heart. There is special joy in reading God's Word and hearing God's voice. Remember that at the heart of Bible reading is our relationship with Jesus. Remember how the Lord opened the Scriptures to the two downcast disciples who were on their way to Emmaus but failed to recognise Him. Later, after they recognised Him, they recollected the experience and remarked, "Were not our hearts burning within us while he talked with us on the road and opened the Scriptures to us?" (Luke 24:32). This is the joy of reading the Bible in His presence, and of hearing His voice.

Our reading of God's Word is made further joyful when our reading and understanding is turned into obedience. When Jesus spoke to His disciples about the vine and its fruit-bearing branches, He remarked, "I have told you this so that my joy may be in you and that your joy may be complete" (John 15:11). What is this that would help to bring fullness to our joy? The answer is in what Jesus had just said in verse 10, "If you obey my commands, you will remain in my love, just as I have obeyed my Father's commands and remain in his love." Here Jesus connects the fullness of joy, obedience and remaining in Him. As for Bible reading, it means that when we allow the words of Christ to remain in our hearts and we obey those words, then our joy that begins with Bible reading will be made complete.

There is a special joy in obeying God and His Word. The joy comes from knowing that in obeying God, we have brought delight and joy to God's heart, and in that knowledge our joy is made complete. It is seeing the smile on God's face, so to speak, that brings the fullness of joy. Here again, we must recognise that joy has to do with relationship. Jesus was eager to bring the joy in His disciples to completeness and fullness, if we were to observe His conversations with His Father and His disciples (John 15:11; 16:24; 17:13). This fullness of joy is often specially connected with suffering. It is the joy of obedience.

At times this joy of obedience will be tested by suffering.

Suffering and Joy

Suffering often comes to us when we seek to obey God, because in doing the will of God we would often have to crucify the sinful flesh and the demands, methods, goals, and fashions of this sinful world. Strangely, it is in suffering to obey God that we find depths of joy otherwise unknown to us. We can find no better model for this than our Lord Himself. He suffered joyfully because He knew that in suffering while obeying His Father, He was bringing glory and delight to His Father. This is brought out by the writer of Hebrews: "Let us fix our eyes on Jesus, the author and perfecter of our faith, who for the joy set before him endured the cross, scorning its shame, and sat down at the right hand of the throne of God" (Hebrews 12:2). Note the confluence of joy and suffering.

When we suffer for obeying God, we know that God is accomplishing His purposes and finishing His work of salvation in us. Therefore we can rejoice that He is delighted with His growing success in us. Peter speaks about this when he wrote:

> "In all this you greatly *rejoice*, though now for a little while you may have had to *suffer grief* in all kinds of trials. These have come so that the proven genuineness of your faith—of greater worth than gold, which perishes even though refined by fire—may result in praise, glory and honor when Jesus Christ is revealed. Though you have not seen him, you love him; and even though you do not see him now, you believe in him and are *filled with an inexpressible and glorious joy*, for you are receiving the end result of your faith, the *salvation of your souls*" (1 Peter 1:6-9, emphasis added).

When we suffer *for* Christ, we also suffer *with* Him. Suffering in this way brings us very close to Jesus, who suffered for us and suffers with us. Paul referred to this experience as "the fellowship of sharing in his [Christ's] sufferings" (Philippians 2:10). It is a sweet fellowship unknown in other circumstances of life because it helps to deepen our relationship with Jesus and heightens our joy in Him.

Usually, our first response when suffering looms in our sunny horizons is to send urgent distress signals to God, bringing to His immediate notice what appear to us to be our deteriorating circumstances. This is quite natural as we want to have happy circumstances. But God has promised us not happy circumstances but to make our souls holy and our salvation complete. This is "the end result of your faith" mentioned by Peter. We should therefore understand why "Prayer changes me" is more important than "Prayer changes things."

God is far more interested in changing our character than our circumstances. Therefore, when potential suffering looms in the horizon, we must learn to focus on the right places so that God can fulfil all His purposes and plans for us. We must seek His *company* more than physical or circumstantial *comfort*, His relationship more than our own success and safety. God will not hesitate to do all that is necessary to change us, the foundations of our lives and the directions of our journeys, until we reflect more and more the character of Christ.

Joy in Our Relationship with Others

Many of the things we have said about the joy that is found in our relationship with God can also be said about our relationships with others. The joy in life comes from relationships. When our relationships with others are affected by sin, and we are alienated from others, our joy is also affected. Our joy is restored when broken relationships are restored through reconciliation, when confession and forgiveness are practised.

Jesus often emphasised the importance of forgiving one another. When asked how many times one should forgive a repetitively offending brother, Jesus answered "seventy times seven" meaning "for as long as he offends" (Matthew 18:22, ESV). In a parable He told of receiving forgiveness from God and learning to forgive others, Jesus offered the case of a servant who is forgiven a huge debt by his master and then goes about to put his fellow servant in jail for a relatively tiny debt (Matthew 18:21-35). This servant did not truly appreciate what was forgiven him, and did not have the joy of having his relationship with his master restored. He was a stranger to the joy of restored relationships; hence his unforgiving and uncouth response to his fellow-servant.

What a joy we experience when we mutually forgive one another for the offences we commit. When we have reconciled and restored relationships, we can find joy — whether it is at home, in the office, in church or in the wider society. "How good and pleasant it is when brothers live together in unity!" (Psalm 133:1).

Such joy in our relationships with others comes from the love that should mark these relationships, in obedience to God, who has commanded us to love one another and our neighbours. With this God-given love, we can rejoice to see the success of others instead of being locked up in envy and anger. Our joy will be heightened especially when we see those who are close to us prosper in the ways of God (2 John 4). Jesus was filled with joy when He spent time with His disciples and saw them respond to God's love and truth. When He saw them mature in their faith and obedience, He rejoiced.

We see the same kind of joy in Paul, who connected his joy with his relationship with his spiritual brothers and sisters. He referred to his fellow believers as "my joy and crown" (Philippians 4:1). Whenever he prayed for them, he prayed with thanksgiving and joy (Philippians 1:3-5). His relationships with fellow Christians brought such joy to Paul's heart. He urged them to live in unity of heart and mind so that his joy could be made complete (Philippians 2:2). In all of this, the emphasis is on restored, right and healthy relationships, mutual respect, regard, concern, and love. There is no place for pride and selfish ambition (Philippians 2:3-4). Such a quality in our relationships will bring forth the joy of the Spirit.

This joy in interpersonal relationships comes from the love that we have for one another — this love comes from God and is established in our relationship with God as God pours His love into our hearts. This love, then, can overflow in our relationships and bring joy with it. Paul wrote to his friend and Christian brother Philemon, "Your love has given me great joy and encouragement" (Philemon 7).

In practical terms, we have already seen what love in our various relationships would be like. When we pray for others, and discern their needs and ask for God's wisdom to meet those needs, we derive much joy when we go about to bring encouragement and edification in their lives through our words, presence and loving deeds. We will feel the joy; so will those who relate with us. This is particularly important in an age where everything is packaged in terms of entertainment paradigms. In the modern era where we are amusing ourselves to death, it is important to know the difference between joy, happiness, and pleasure, and to pursue the joy that will outlast everything else because it is rooted in the eternal God.

Questions for Reflection

1. Discuss the differences between pleasure, happiness and joy. Why is it important to pursue joy more than the others? In what way is joy essentially relational in nature?

2. What can we learn from Jesus about joy? What did He teach about joy and how did He show joy in His life and ministry?

3. Why is there joy in God's presence (Psalm 21:6)? What can we do in God's presence that will bring joy to us? How can this joy be expressed in our other relationships?

4. What is the connection between suffering and joy? What evidence do you find in Scripture that it is possible to be joyful even in suffering? Share from your own experience how this is possible.

6

PEACE: LOVE AT REST

Peace is something that is widely desired. Nations and communities torn by violence and war long for peace that would give them breathing space and allow them to live lives in relative calm. Families subject to tensions, abuse and misunderstandings long for some peace so that there may be some measure of happiness in their lives. The same can be said for communities and neighbourhoods of all kinds. Above all, in the human heart there is a longing for personal peace in the midst of relentless competitiveness in a demanding and rapidly changing world. An oasis of peace is what many long for when they go for a holiday (though many holidays turn out to be not as peaceful as one would have hoped) or attend meditation classes. But peace is often elusive. How can one find peace?

To find our answer we must turn to Jesus, whose birth was prophesied by the prophet Isaiah in the early 7th century BC, and whose name was declared to be the "Prince of Peace" (Isaiah 9:6). At His birth, a choir of angels appeared to sing, "Glory to God in the highest, and on earth peace to men on whom his favor rests" (Luke 2:14). His turning up on earth had to do with bringing peace to earth and the people of this world. It is therefore not surprising that He often greeted people with "Peace be with you." When He spoke to His disciples before being sacrificed on the cross, He reassured His disciples with many encouraging words.

He promised them peace. "Peace I leave with you; my peace I give you. I do not give to you as the world gives. Do not let your hearts be troubled and do not be afraid" (John 14:27). After His death and resurrection, Jesus appeared to His disciples and greeted them with "Peace be with you!" (John 20:19, 26; Luke 24:36). He then sent His disciples into the world to proclaim the message of peace which He would bring to all who would believe.

The Longing for Peace

The biblical narrative begins with how peace was lost: in the heart of man when he sinned against God, in the Garden of Eden when God was disobeyed, in the first marriage when Adam and Eve blamed each other for their troubles, in the first family when Cain murdered his brother Abel, and in the world when nations fought against one another.

Then God called one man — Abraham — and brought him to the promised land, promising to bless him and his descendants so that they will be a blessing to the nations. A long and chequered story of Abraham's descendents followed, from wandering shepherds to slavery in Egypt, exodus and freedom in the promised land, and the establishment of a kingdom, from success to failure, from faithfulness to apostasy. In the entire story, God is in the picture, working out His eternal purposes. There is a continuous ray of hope that peace will be found at last.

Aaron, the high priest and brother of Moses, was taught by God on how to bless the people of Israel. "The LORD bless you and keep you; the LORD make his face to shine upon you and be gracious to you; the LORD turn his face toward you and give you peace" (Numbers 6:26). The Aaronic blessing blesses people with God's peace; the word used here is a richly wonderful Hebrew word — *shalom*. *Shalom* referred to the rich quality of the biblical concept of peace. It refers not only to trouble-free circumstances, but also to the quality of relationship and the welfare of people. In addition, it refers to ideas of wholeness and wellness, safety and soundness. Even the animals are included in this concept of *shalom* (see Genesis 37:14, where Jacob sends his son Joseph to check out his brothers who were out grazing their flock; he was asked to check on the *shalom* of his brothers as well as their flocks).

This *shalom* is given by God. He promised His people, "I will grant peace in the land, and you will lie down and no one will make you afraid" (Leviticus 26:6). God's covenant with His people is a covenant of peace (Numbers 25:12; Isaiah 54:10). The literature of the Old Testament points to this peace as an ideal to be hoped for and pursued. The Psalmists sang about this peace. Pilgrims to Jerusalem were urged to pray for the peace of the holy city of God on earth (Psalm 122:6). The worshippers sang about the salvation of God and of the connection between righteousness and peace (Psalm 85:10).

One cannot expect God's peace when continuing in unrighteousness and wickedness. God's peace is for the righteous. Thus people are urged to "seek peace and pursue it" (which for most people would be a perfectly acceptable injunction) but it is connected with the injunction "Turn from evil and do good" (Psalm 34:14). Peace is not a commodity that one can pick and choose from the spiritual supermarket. It is always connected with righteousness, holiness and faithfulness. Therefore, the Lord has declared that "That there is no peace…for the wicked" (Isaiah 48:22).

This is one of the reasons why Israel did not see much of the wonderful peace that was promised by God. They made the conditions for the peace into fine print that few bothered to read. They became presumptuous about their relationship with God, assuming they were guaranteed peace. The Lord complained about the prophets and priests who, being unfaithful to Him, ended up as spiritual masseurs: "'They dress the wound of my people as though it were not serious. "'Peace, peace,' they say, when there is no peace" (Jeremiah 6:14). They failed to remind people that they could not have peace without taking care of their relationship with God, who had made a covenant of peace with them. The loss of peace in Israel is recorded in the long and tragic history of its people: the apostasy, wars, defeats, exile, shame and foreign domination.

In the midst of such apostasy and the loss of peace, there was still a longing for the peace that God had promised. A remnant of teaching that urged people to pursue the peace that comes through faithfulness to God was preserved throughout the nation's history. But such peace had to wait for the coming of the Prince of Peace.

The Fulfilment of Peace

When Jesus came to this world, He brought with Him His peace — a peace that came with a heavy price. The peace of Jesus had to do with His atoning sacrifice on the cross. Paul tells us that Jesus "Himself is our peace" (Ephesians 2:14). Writing to the Gentiles, he reminded them of how they were "without hope and without God in the world" but that in Christ now they who "were far away have been brought near through the blood of Christ" (Ephesians 2:12-13).

The atoning sacrifice of Jesus has brought us peace with God (Romans 5:1) by reconciling us with God and removing the guilt of our sins. He has covered us and our shame with His righteousness, and thus has brought us both His righteousness and the peace that accompanies it. It is in this way that peace has come to our hearts.

The Christian life is a call to live in peace, and this is possible if we live in Christ. Jesus said, "I have told you these things, so that in me you may have peace" (John 16:33). In Christ, we have peace with God and others. Paul picks up this point when he wrote that Christ is our peace (between the Jews and the Gentiles) and that in the church, he has "destroyed the barrier, the dividing wall of hostility" so that both, to whom he preached peace, can be reconciled and find peace in Christ (Ephesians 2:14-17).

We have thus seen that the peace that God had promised has to do with faithfulness to God and righteousness. Its reception, though longed for by many, had to wait till it was fulfilled by Christ. The Lord is our peace — he paid the penalty for our sins and reconciled us with God. In that peace with God, we can find peace with one another. This peace is an outcome of our living in Christ and the work of the indwelling Holy Spirit. We can experience this peace in increasing measures and mediate it to others. Such peace is the fruit of the Holy Spirit.

Horatius Bonar has shown that peace and holiness are closely related in the preface of his most helpful book, *God's Way of Holiness* (written in the 19th century):

> "The way of peace and the way of holiness lie side by side, or rather, they are one. That which bestows the one imparts the other; and he who takes the one takes the other also. The Spirit of peace is the Spirit of holiness. The God of peace is the God of holiness.
>
> If at any time these paths seem to go asunder, there must be something wrong — wrong in the teaching that makes them seem to part company, or wrong in the state of the man in whose life they have done so.
>
> They start together, or at least so nearly together that no eye, save the divine, can mark a difference. Yet, properly speaking, the peace goes before the holiness, and is its parent. This is what divines call 'priority in nature, though not in time,' which means substantially this, that the difference in such almost identical beginnings is too small in point of time to be perceived by us, yet it is not on that account the less distinct and real.
>
> The two are not independent. There is fellowship between them, vital fellowship, each being the helpmeet of the other. The fellowship is not of mere coincidence, as in the case of strangers who happen to meet on the same path, nor of arbitrary appointment, as in the case of two parallel roads, but of mutual help and sympathy — like the fellowship of head and heart, or of two members of one body, the peace being indispensable to the production or causation of the holiness, and the holiness indispensable to the maintaining and deepening of the peace…(T)rue holiness must start from a true and authentic peace."[1]

Peace with God is the fertile ground on which holiness grows. This is a doctrinal as well as practical truth on which we must guide our steps of discipleship. It does tell us that both peace and holiness are relational realities.

The original Greek word, *eirēnē*, is probably derived from the verb *eiro* which means "to join." This helps us to understand that peace is relational. It refers to the tranquillity and wellbeing that comes from healthy relationships. This peace is a gift from God.

The question is how can we live out this peace.

Living out the Peace

The peace that is a gift of God and the fruit of the Spirit is received by us through faith as God graciously blesses us. In this, Jesus is not only our Saviour but also our Model. On earth, He walked with peace and poise. He had a perfect relationship with the Father and had a loving relationship with others that brought peace to many of them. Jesus did not just passively do nothing to live out this peace. He in fact had habits that we must learn from.

Peace with God

Unlike any of us, Jesus did not sin — he was the sinless one. His relationship with His Father was intimate and without any barrier. Yet He found it necessary to find time alone with His Father, and He did this frequently — not because of some anxiety that his Father would forget Him if He did not, but because He immensely loved His Father. It was impossible for Him to spend any day without communion with His Father.

Regular Confession

Unlike Jesus, every one of us is a sinner. Our ongoing sins often get in the way of our relationship with God even after we have been saved by believing in Jesus. We have already seen in chapter 5 that it is important to establish a habit of regular repentance and confession of sin. It is impossible to grow in Christ and reflect His character unless repentance is a frequent part of our devotional lives.

Gary Thomas has written of the process of spiritual transformation linked with surrendering to God as a "beautiful fight." "If I recognize that I am not like Christ, that I am proud where he is humble, that I am selfish where he is sacrificial, that I am greedy where he is giving, that I am lustful where he is pure, then mustn't I be broken before I can be remade?"[2]

Repentance is linked with transformation. It also brings peace and deepens our relationship with God. If we go on sinning, we will lose both the joy and peace that are connected with the loving relationship we are called to have with God. This is essential if we are to enjoy the peace that comes from a clear conscience and a loving relationship with God, not muddied by unconfessed sin.

Ready Obedience

As we have seen previously, love for God is shown through our ready obedience. It is this obedience that also brings God's peace into our lives. Often, our self-will will resist and wrestle against God but when we submit to God's will, we will have an immense peace that comes from beyond us.

Besides regular confession and obeying God, an important factor in keeping the peace that God has given us is learning to trust Him.

Trusting God

Trusting God is difficult for people who are trained to fend for themselves in a highly competitive world; or who have learned to calculate everything and become calculative. Trusting God is extremely difficult for people surrounded by others who have let them down or whom they believe will let them down.

We learn to trust God by knowing Him. Here doctrine is important because unfortunately, for many, doctrine has been sidelined. Their idea of God is often distorted with their own ideas and experiences. God is a collage of the best and the worst experiences in one's life. However, if we truly want to know God, we have to turn to where God has revealed Himself — in the Word of God, His Son Jesus, and in the continuing ministry of the Holy Spirit who brings us to God and Jesus.

J. I. Packer's *Knowing God* and A. W. Tozer's *The Knowledge of the Holy* are classics that turn our attention to the character of God.[3] They point us to the need for a robust study of who God is to feed into our relationship with God. We will then discover that what God says He is, He will demonstrate in our daily relationship. The more we get to know this God, the more we can get to trust Him. The more we trust Him, the more His peace will fill our hearts. As the prophet Isaiah testified to God, "Thou wilt keep him in perfect peace, *whose mind is stayed on thee*: because he trusteth in thee" (Isaiah 26:3, KJV, emphasis added).

Jesus was the living example of this. He showed this tremendous peace in His daily routines. He did face numerous enemies who were out to make life extremely difficult for Him, and who were plotting to kill Him. He also had many other challenges and the needs of masses of people that were brought to His attention. In all of this He walked in perfect peace because He trusted His Father. He encouraged His listeners to likewise trust His Father. He told them not to worry about the many needs of life such as food and clothes.

> "For the pagans run after all these things, and your heavenly Father knows that you need them. But seek first his kingdom and his righteousness, and all these things will be given to you as well. Therefore do not worry about tomorrow, for tomorrow will worry about itself. Each day has enough trouble of its own" (Matthew 6:32-34).

To focus on God, to know and trust Him — this is the relationship that brings true peace into our hearts so that even in the uncertainties in life, we can have peace that cannot be shaken. Psalm 112 speaks about the righteous man who fears the Lord: "He will have no fear of bad news; his heart is steadfast, trusting in the Lord" (Psalm 112:7). Such is the unshakeable peace through the uncertain circumstances of a man who knows His God and trusts in Him.

There is an old-fashioned word used by many Christian writers of old. It is the word "resignation" — it does not refer to a sense of giving up because of a fatalistic view of life. Neither does it equate to "whatever", in today's language, or "whatever will be will be." Rather, it refers to the example of Christ who prayed at the Garden of Gethsemane, "not as I will but as you will" (Matthew 26:39). To resign to the ways of God is to actively believe that His will is superior to mine. I resign as the master of my life and hand over the steering wheel to God, the true Master of my life. It is not fatalism but an active response to the character and promises of God. It arises from trusting God.

Charles Spurgeon connects such resignation with peace, the fruit of the Spirit:

> "The habit of resignation is the root of peace. A godly child has a ring given him by his mother, and he greatly prized it, but on a sudden he unhappily lost his ring, and he cried bitterly. Recollecting himself, he stepped aside and prayed; after which his sister laughingly said to him, 'Brother, what is the good of praying about a ring? Will praying bring back your ring?' 'No,' said he, 'sister, perhaps not, but praying has done this for me, it has made me quite willing to do without the ring if it is God's will; and is not that almost as good as having it?'
>
> This faith quiets us by resignation, as a babe is hushed in his mother's bosom. Faith makes us quite willing without the mercy which once was prized; and when the heart is content to be without the outward blessing, it is happy as it would be with it; for it is at rest."[4]

Such trust in God will see itself bringing all needs and challenges to God in prayer. Having brought these matters to God in prayer, we can then rest assured that God knows and will do what is necessary according to His will. And all that He does is for our good, Scripture assures us (Romans 8:28). Therefore, we do well by heeding the biblical instructions and promises concerning trust, prayer and peace:

> "Do not be anxious about anything, but in every situation, by prayer and petition, with thanksgiving, present your requests to God. And the peace of God, which transcends all understanding, will guard your hearts and your minds in Christ Jesus" (Philippians 4:6-7).

Others may find it difficult to understand such peace that comes from trusting God and laying everything down at His feet in prayer. Even we ourselves may not understand our own response and demeanour. This peace is truly beyond understanding because it comes from God. It will fill our entire beings (our hearts and minds) and bring peace to us. We will then be enabled to walk our paths with peace and poise.

Peace with Others

We are called to live the Christian life by seeking and bringing peace to others. Because the essence of Christian living is relational — vertically and horizontally — it is marked by love and the peace that accompanies it.

Peace in the Church

This is most possible within the setting of a church which is a community of redeemed individuals. We are to love one another and show that love by forgiving each other's offences. When we come together at the Lord's Table, it is customary to exchange signs of reconciliation and peace after we have confessed our sins and received the forgiveness of God. Peace between believers is an expectation of God when His children gather to worship Him. It would be difficult to worship God and sing about our joy and peace in Him when our relationships with other believers are strained.

To be sure it is not always easy to be at peace with everyone. Even if you are open to someone, he may be hostile or closed to you. But as Scripture exhorts us, we are to "Live in harmony with one another" (Romans 12:16). Paul is aware of difficulties in real life but he places the responsibility in our own courts when he writes, "If it is possible, as far as it depends on *you*, live at peace with *everyone*" (Romans 12:18, emphasis added). Our peace with others must reach as widely as possible, and it must be strengthened by our own initiatives rather than by waiting for others.

If we understand this, then we would also understand why Jesus emphasised reconciliation and peace between believers when they come to worship God. In God's eyes, making peace is more important than offering sacrifices in worship: "Therefore, if you are offering your gift at the altar and there remember that your brother has something against you, leave your gift there in front of the altar. First go and be reconciled to your brother; then come and offer your gift" (Matthew 5:23-24). God, like every parent, wishes to see peace among His children; we also know that God's children are peacemakers (Matthew 5:9). But experience tells us that we do not always succeed in this. Some things get in the way.

Self-interest, selfishness, pride, one-upmanship are often common causes for divisions and relational tensions in church. Immaturity and worldliness in the members of the church can lead to a focus on non-important things leading to unnecessary fights and sometimes tragic and shameful results. Even the early church saw signs of this in some places because of the ubiquitous sinful self. "Brothers, I could not address you as spiritual but as worldly — mere infants in Christ...You are still worldly. For since there is jealousy and quarrelling among you, are you not worldly? Are you not acting like mere men?" (1 Corinthians 3:1-3). Paul's words to the Corinthians were written with a sense of frustration and grief. In his appeal he urged them to grow up and recognise how childish their behaviour was, which had robbed the church of its peace and brought dishonour to Christ.

The former United Nations Secretary General, Dag Hammarskjöld, who left behind profoundly reflective writings, wrote of how we can escape selfishness and self-centredness and find peace if we prayed the Lord's Prayer well:

> "Hallowed be Your name,
>   *not mine*,
> Your kingdom come,
>   *not mine*,
> Your will be done,
>   *not mine*,
> Give us peace with You
> Peace with others
> Peace with ourselves
> And free us from fear."[5]

Often, peace among believers is easily lost when we are too quick to judge each other, especially in matters of opinion (which are blown up to doctrinal proportions). The Christians in Rome had disputes regarding the proper Christian response to the issue of food that had been offered to idols. Are Christians permitted to eat such food? Paul urged the believers to accept each other "without passing judgment on disputable matters" — "The man who eats everything must not look down on him who does not, and the man who does not eat everything must not condemn the man who does, for God has accepted him" (Romans 12:1-3). There are two problems noted here: hasty judgment, and exercising such judgmentalism on unimportant matters. How true this can be in the church!

When exposing our human foibles, Jesus sometimes injects humour when putting it across: "Why do you look at the speck of sawdust in your brother's eye and pay no attention to the plank in your own eye" (Matthew 7:4)? What a funny sight, but it is tragically sad too when it becomes the hallmark of a church. Such a church may sing about peace but there will be no peace.

In the case of the church quarrelling and arguing over food (that had been offered to idols) Paul declared that "the Kingdom of God is not a matter of eating and drinking, but of righteousness, peace and joy in the Holy Spirit" (Romans 14:17). Paul is saying that we should get down to the things that really matter in church — such as righteousness (which has to do with right and healthy relationships, vertically and horizontally) and peace and joy (which are based on such right relationships). Peace and joy are part of the fruit of the Holy Spirit, and we have been reiterating that they have to do with relationships. Maintaining right peaceful relationships is more important than arguing about matters of opinion and issues that will not be the highlight of any discussion we may have in heaven one day.

Peace in the Family

What is true in church is also true in family life. What we had said earlier about family relationships and the need for love in them needs to be reiterated here. Only when such relationships are present will there by joy and peace. For peace to be in the family, there must be lots of understanding, mutual forgiveness and reconciliation. The self must be dethroned and Christ enthroned. Mutual love, understanding, respect and submission will go a long way in building the experience of peace in the family.

Peace in Society

Similar principles apply in our relationships with those outside the family and church. The injunction, "Make every effort to live in peace with *all men* and to be holy" (Hebrews 12:14, emphasis added) must be considered seriously. There are two areas in which we must not spare any effort — our growth in holiness and our peaceful relationships. Note that we are to seek peace with all men. This means you can make a list of all the people you know or come across, and everyone should be on your peacemaking list. No one should be excluded.

In reality not everyone would be interested or inclined to live peacefully with us — the inconsiderate driver on the road, the boorish neighbour who throws his rubbish into your garden, the bossy colleague who is working to create trouble for you at the workplace. But we are still to do our very best to maintain peace. Sometimes we will fail because of the other party. Jesus had His own detractors who refused to see eye to eye with Him and who plotted to dispose of Him. He could not live in peace with them. Yet He prayed for them on the cross. His heart was in the right place though the circumstances were working against Him.

Sometimes we may be persecuted by others for our faith and for living faithfully before God. In some countries this is a real and serious problem. The early church was no stranger to harsh treatment by hostile neighbours. Even in such circumstances, the biblical advice is to seek peace by not making things worse and by displaying the very character of Christ. Peter, in writing to a persecuted church, advised his fellow believers, "Always be prepared to give an answer to everyone who asks you to give the reason for the hope that you have. But do this with gentleness and respect, keeping a clear conscience, so that those who speak maliciously against your good behavior in Christ may be ashamed of their slander" (1 Peter 3:15-16). He encouraged the believers to live honourable lives that are faithful to God and reflective of the beauty of Christ's character: "Live such good lives among the pagans that, though they accuse you of doing wrong, they may see your good deeds and glorify God on the day he visits us" (1 Peter 2:12).

In evangelism, Christians should refrain from causing unnecessary offence and hostility, for example by running down other people's religious practices or religions. We should simply preach Christ and lift Him high in our sharing (John 12:32). We should be like the one we are preaching about.

Christians should also be involved in their larger community as they "seek the welfare of the city" (Jeremiah 27:9, ESV) and meet the needs of the poor, the marginalised, and those who need other forms of help. In doing good in the community, we will earn goodwill that will go a long way in building peaceful relationships with our neighbours. In the context of these relationships we can share Christ. There is no place for haughty arrogance or uncaring isolation on our part.

Peace is Relational

We conclude by noting again that the fruit of the Spirit has to do with the relational dimensions of our lives. Therefore, peace is also something that has to do with our relationships. People who cut themselves off by hoarding their wealth for their own self-consumption, or try to live their lives independent of God cannot have the peace promised by God.

Peace is a supernatural fruit given to us by God. It grows out of our lives when we seek to be reconciled with God and others, when we seek to love God with all our powers and to love our neighbours. This peace is not the absence of troubles or difficult circumstances. In fact such divine peace is often experienced in the noise and dust of human life, not in some imaginary luxury island.

A competition was once held to find the perfect picture of peace and received wide interest from artists. The judges unveiled painting after painting, and they were all admirable. Finally there were two left. One was a painting of a peaceful pastoral scene, with a placid lake, beautiful evening sky, grassy shore and sheep peacefully feeding there. Everyone thought this was surely the winner until the last painting was unveiled. Everybody gasped.

> "A tumultuous waterfall cascaded down a rocky precipice; the crowd could almost feel its cold, penetrating spray. Stormy-gray clouds threatened to explode with lightning, wind and rain. In the midst of the thundering noises and bitter chill, a spindly tree clung to the rocks at the edge of the falls. One of its branches reached out in front of the torrential waters as if foolishly seeking to experience its full power.
>
> A little bird had built a nest in the elbow of that branch. Content and undisturbed in her stormy surroundings, she rested on her eggs. With her eyes closed and her wings ready to cover her little ones, she manifested peace that transcends all earthly turmoil."[6]

This winning painting deeply and powerfully represents true peace, the kind that is described and promised in the Bible. Such peace is not measured by the absence of disturbance or trouble, simply because it arises from our relationship with God rather than from our circumstances. This peace has a depth that amazes and surprises, for it draws its strength and sturdiness from our response of trust in the promises of the God who has demonstrated again and again that He is faithful.

If our life is *in* Christ, we will find this peace (John 16:33), and we will be able to walk with peace and poise, and bring this peace to as many of our relationships as possible.

Questions for Reflection

1. What does the Bible say about *shalom*? In what way has it already been realised and in what way is it yet to be fully realised?

2. Read Isaiah 26:3. How are thinking about God, trusting in Him, and enjoying peace all connected with each other? Why do people find it difficult to trust God? How can they learn to trust Him more? What would be the results?

3. Is it possible to live at peace with everyone (Romans 12:18)? If not, what is the problem? How can you do something more to build peace with others?

4. In what way is peace an essentially relational and a supernatural fruit? Can one be peaceful even in troubling circumstances? How would this be possible?

7

PATIENCE: WHEN MATURE LOVE WAITS

You may have heard of the urgent prayer of a Christian: "Lord, give me patience, and give it to me *now*!" Patience is an increasingly rare commodity these days in our increasingly impatient culture, driven by immediate demands for instant gratification and powered by technology that is designed to eliminate the need for patience in our lives.

Short Fuses and Long Noses

Paul says that patience is a characteristic of the fruit of the Holy Spirit. The Greek word in the original text is *makrothumia* which literally means "long-souled." It comes from *makran* (meaning "far off") and *thumos* (meaning "fierceness or indignation"). It "speaks of the steadfastness of the soul under provocation" and "includes the idea of forbearance and a patient endurance of wrong under ill-treatment, without anger of thought or thought of revenge."[1]

Similar concepts are conveyed by parallel Hebrew words in the Old Testament.[2] The Hebrew phrase *erech apayim* literally means "long of nose" and is used as a divine characteristic as well as the mark of a righteous and wise person. God is described as "slow to anger" (Exodus 34:6; Psalm 103:8; Nahum 1:3), which literally means to be "long-nosed." In modern idiom, we would say God has a "long fuse", that is, he is not short-tempered. Likewise, a wise godly person would also be "long-nosed" like God. "A person's wisdom yields patience; it is to one's glory to overlook an offense" (Proverbs 19:11).

Another idea that is closely related to the idea of patience is endurance. If patience is primarily "the capacity to be 'long-minded', to delay making a response to provocative people"[3] then endurance (or steadfastness) has to do with facing adverse and difficult circumstances calmly and without losing hope. The Greek word in the New Testament that is translated as endurance or steadfastness is *hupomonē*. Paul wrote about his patience and endurance: "You, however, know all about my teaching, my way of life, my purpose, faith, patience, love, endurance, persecutions, sufferings — what kinds of things happened to me in Antioch, Iconium and Lystra, the persecutions I endured. Yet the Lord rescued me from all of them" (2 Timothy 3:10-11).

Scripture has much to teach about patience. Consider the following verses from Psalms (ESV):

> "Indeed, none who wait for you shall be put to shame... Lead me in your truth and teach me, for you are the God of my salvation; for you I wait all the day long...May integrity and uprightness preserve me, for I wait for you" (Psalm 25:2, 5, 21).
>
> "Wait for the Lord; be strong, and let your heart take courage; wait for the Lord!" (Psalm 27:14).
>
> "Be still before the LORD and wait patiently for him; fret not yourself over the one who prospers in his way, over the man who carries out evil devices!...Wait for the LORD and keep his way, and he will exalt you to inherit the land; you will look on when the wicked are cut off" (Psalm 37:7, 34).
>
> "For God alone, O my soul, wait in silence, for my hope is from him" (Psalm 62:5).

The quality of patience has to do with both how we deal with difficult people and difficult circumstances. It has to do with being "long-nosed" in the midst of unlovely people and having a high tolerance for difficult circumstances. We know from personal experience that there is something supernatural in being able to exercise patience and endurance in this way. To understand this as well as exhibit this patience, we must turn to Jesus.

The Patience of Jesus

Jesus is remembered for His patience by those who knew Him — His eyewitnesses. For example, John in his old age especially mentions the patience of Jesus Christ: "I John, who also am your brother, and companion in tribulation, and in the kingdom and *patience of Jesus Christ*, was in the isle that is called Patmos, for the word of God, and for the testimony of Jesus Christ" (Revelation 1:9, KJV, emphasis added). To be sure, John could remember, in his interactions with Jesus and in observing Jesus relating with and ministering to people, the many instances when he witnessed the patience of Jesus towards people in the most difficult of circumstances.

As an apostle, Paul also had encounters with the Lord Jesus, although his interactions with Jesus were all presumably after the resurrection of Jesus (Acts 9). Paul, unlike John, did not seem to have had any personal encounter with Jesus before the cross. Nevertheless, Jesus chose to interact with him in a special way as to qualify him to be an apostle (as a special witness of Jesus arising from direct encounters with Him). Paul certainly had a close and personal knowledge of Jesus and experienced His Lord in an exceptional way.

Paul characterised His encounters with Jesus as one full of grace on the part of Jesus. He wrote, "But for that very reason I was shown mercy so that in me, the worst of sinners, Christ Jesus might display his *immense patience* as an example for those who would believe in him and receive eternal life" (1 Timothy 1:16, emphasis added). Paul testifies to Timothy his protégé that he had experienced the "immense patience" of Jesus in the way Jesus had dealt and related with Him. Paul had good reason to describe Jesus in this way for He knew how he had hunted Christians down, relentlessly pursuing and persecuting them, and what his murderous threats would have felt like to both the Christians and their Lord. But then Jesus patiently dealt with Paul and converted him. For many decades, Paul experienced the transforming grace of Jesus and knew how patient Jesus had been with him.

In all of this, Jesus was displaying the very character of God (for He Himself was God). God, Scripture asserts, is rich in patience (Romans 2:14), a quality we see described throughout the Bible. In the Gospels we see how Jesus exercised patience both in terms of people and circumstances.

Jesus had Patience for His Disciples

Surrounded by people who were spiritually ignorant and slow to grasp things, it is amazing how greatly Jesus showed quiet patience. At one time, Jesus was teaching His disciples in private, and explaining to them how He would die and be raised from the dead. The disciples did not grasp what He had said — "But they did not understand what he meant and were afraid to ask him about it" (Mark 9:30-32). Instead they had arguments on the road to Capernaum even as they were following Him. Jesus knew what they were arguing about and as it turned out it was about who among them was the greatest (Mark 9:33-34). How grossly off the mark they were! Was Jesus simply throwing in vain "pearls to pigs" (Matthew 7:6)? It takes great patience for a teacher to teach extremely slow pupils.

Before this incident described in Mark's Gospel, Jesus took the inner circle of His disciples — Peter, James and John — up a mountain to witness His transfiguration. There they saw the transfigured Jesus together with Moses and Elijah. What a sight it must have been. Peter, with his usual impulsive ways, immediately suggested that three shelters be put up, one each for Jesus and His two companions who were once dead but now were alive. Mark says that Peter "did not know what to say" (Mark 9:9). Peter ended up saying something rather meaningless and foolish. Matthew's account suggests that Peter rudely interrupted the conversation that Jesus was having with the two visitors; God had to interrupt Peter's silly outburst by declaring the identity of Jesus and commanding the disciples to listen to Him (Matthew 17:3-5).

After such an exhilarating experience, Jesus told the disciples as they were coming down the mountain that the Son of Man would rise from the dead. Again, they displayed a frustrating failure to understand: "They kept the matter to themselves, discussing what 'rising from the dead' meant" (Mark 9:10). And this just after they had seen the ancient characters of Moses and Elijah!

There were many other occasions when Jesus had to exercise patience in teaching and dealing with the ignorance and spiritual slowness of His disciples (John 14:6-10; Mark 6:35-37; Luke 22:36-38; John 20:24-29 — just to name a few examples).

Jesus had Patience at Home

Jesus had the same patience for His family. When He was 12, He visited the temple in Jerusalem with His parents. The parents left for home with friends and relatives without Jesus and did not realise He was not with them. After finding Him some days later, Mary (perhaps with a note of irritation in her voice) asked Jesus why He had treated His parents poorly. Whose fault was it really? In His reply Jesus said something profound about His identity, referring to being in His Father's house. Scripture tells us that the parents "did not understand what he was saying to them." And yet, Jesus "went down to Nazareth with them and was obedient to them" (Luke 2:41-51). He had patience for parents who were slow to understand.

His family at times doubted His sanity and tried to "rescue" Him (Mark 3:21). He had problems convincing His own relatives as to who He was (Mark 6:4-6). And yet, besides Mary, two of His brothers (James and Jude, both of whom contributed to the New Testament) became key leaders of the early church. Jesus had much patience at home too.

Jesus had Patience for His Enemies

Jesus not only had patience for relatives, friends and disciples. Amazingly He also showed great patience for His enemies. He had many detractors, some of whom viciously made life extremely difficult for Him. They tried to trap Him with trick questions. They spread rumours about Him. They plotted to kill Him. Yet Jesus was patient with them. In the words of Charles Edward Jefferson, "This Man of Galilee knew little but misunderstanding and ingratitude and criticism and abuse; but he never complained and at the end of the day he was as sweet as at dawn."[4]

When Jesus was in the synagogue in Nazareth His hometown, the initial positive response of the people turned sour as he told them some unpalatable truths about the narrowness of the Jews' faith and the wideness of God's grace in embracing the Gentiles. They "took him to the brow of the hill...to throw him down the cliff." But Jesus simply "walked right through the crowd and went on his way" (Luke 4:29-30). Jesus had the power, as the Son of God, to wipe out His enemies, but He had patience for them because He came not to flex His divine muscles to destroy but to give Himself up to save friend and foe.

We see this patience of Jesus for His enemies on many other occasions. There was one time when Jesus had a conversation (we can call it a debate) with argumentative Jews who were blinded by their self-righteousness. Some of them initially believed but even they were still blinded by their mistaken thoughts. When Jesus talked about true freedom, they remarked that, being Abraham's descendents, they had never been slaves to anyone (John 8:31-33). This is most incredible, for every Jew would have been taught about the slavery of the Israelites in Egypt and how God rescued them through Moses! Jesus patiently told them the importance of becoming free from sin.

As Jesus taught more and more and revealed His true identity, His listeners became increasingly agitated. Finally, they "picked up stones to stone him, but Jesus hid himself, slipping away from the temple grounds" (John 8:59). Jesus could have rained down huge boulders from the skies on them, but He patiently left because He had a mission to accomplish — it had to do with His love for all, including His enemies and tormentors.

The greatest example of the patience that Jesus showed towards His enemies was His response during His final days on earth. His own disciple Judas was secretly colluding with the enemies of Jesus to betray His whereabouts so that He could be arrested. Jesus knew this and yet patiently washed Judas' dirty and unfaithful feet and ate the Last Supper with him. At His trials, where He was dragged from one place to another in a series of kangaroo courts, He patiently held His peace. When He was charged in court, He "made no reply, not even to a single charge — to the great amazement of the governor" (Matthew 27:14). Jesus was there not to win His court case, but to win the sinful world for His Father.

When Jesus was cruelly mocked and beaten by the rough and uncaring Roman soldiers, He could have lost His patience at such terrible behaviour. Who did they think they were, treating the Creator and Ruler of the universe in such a despicable manner? But Jesus was patient so that He could do what was necessary to save them. He was mocked and spat upon but did not react with anger or vengeance. Many taunted Him to come down from the cross to save Himself with the power He apparently had. But no straw broke the camel's back. The lion held back His power and His full roar. Jesus refused to be provoked. He remained immensely patient till He had finished His Father's work. He even prayed for His enemies, asking the Father to forgive them. Such patience!

Jonathan Edwards describes this amazingly great patience of Jesus at the cross. He paints a portrait of Christ under attack by enemies on earth and from hell. Jesus showed "holy boldness and valour" not in the "exercise of any fiery passions; not in fierce and violent speeches...but in not opening His mouth when afflicted and oppressed...not shedding others' blood, but with all-conquering patience and love shedding his own." Pointing to how Jesus graciously healed the servant of the high priest whose ears angry and impulsive Peter shaved off, Edwards concludes: "Never was the patience, meekness, love, and forgiveness of Christ so gloriously manifest as at that time. Never did He appear so much a Lamb, and never did he show so much of the dove-like spirit as at that time."[5]

Jesus had Patience in Difficult Circumstances

The enemies of Jesus made life very difficult for Jesus — but He was extremely patient in those circumstances. This was surely due to the fact that Jesus had entrusted Himself completely into His Father's hands and was totally committed to doing the Father's will. He trusted His Father and therefore was able to exercise the kind of patience that is profoundly amazing.

It is this patience that enabled Jesus to wait 30 years in relative obscurity before He burst forth in public ministry. Charles Edward Jefferson's powerful words describe well the immense patience of the young Jesus:

> "Think of what delay must have meant to Jesus. How his blood must have boiled in little sleepy Nazareth as he dreamed of the mighty things which ought to be done and which he felt he could do in the great arena. As man after man brushed by him on his way to success and renown his soul must have been agitated, he too must have felt the fever to hasten on. Think of what his dream was and you will understand how it must have tugged at him and made the years seem interminable in drowsy, prosaic Nazareth. But he waited. At twenty-one he said, not yet. At twenty-five, not yet. At twenty-eight, not yet. It is in the twenties that the blood is hottest and the soul is most eager to get on. Through all the blazing years of youth Jesus waited in Nazareth. It was not until he was in his thirtieth year that he said to himself, The time has come."[6]

Why wait 30 years when at the age of 12 Jesus already exhibited such profound knowledge as He held discussions with the religious teachers in the temple? Why spend such long years working as a builder and carpenter for the welfare of His family? The answer is clear — He marked time according to His Father's plans and schedule. Many were the times when He remarked that "the time has not come" (John 2:4, cf. John 7:30; 8:20) when He was urged by others to surge ahead or hurry down the road of impulse, ambition or self-effort. Instead Jesus had a perfect sense of timing as he walked in perfect rhythm with His Father.

Just before He went to the cross, Jesus prayed, "Father, the time has come" and went ahead to glorify His Father by saving the world on the cross (John 17:1). Jesus is the perfect model of waiting for God patiently and obeying at the right time.

When His friend Lazarus died, Jesus waited deliberately for a few days, so much so that His disciples got rather confused about His feelings for His friend or His lack of fear in going to Jerusalem and its neighbourhood. That Jesus did not lack any feelings over the death of Lazarus was proven in the way Jesus wept when He reached Bethany (John 11:35). Jesus patiently delayed His trip to Bethany (against perhaps His natural feelings) for the sake of the disciples (and for all our sakes who read the Gospel account) that we may believe Jesus. Here, too, we see patience displayed for a higher purpose, in accordance with God's script.

The Patient Life

As believers in Jesus, we are called to live with patience as a characteristic of our inner lives and outward relationships. Oswald Chambers has rooted the Christian life of patience in the Christian virtues of faith, hope and love. These virtues in the Spirit-filled life enable believers to be patient. Christians can be patient because they trust God, hope in God, and love God and others. Chambers describes the ways of God in this way:

> "The patience of the saints may be illustrated by the figure of a bow and arrow in the hands of God. He sees the target and takes aim. He strains the bow, not to breaking-point, however severe the strain may seem to the saint, but to just that point whence the arrow will fly with surest, swiftest

> speed to the bull's-eye...The patience of the saints, like the patience of our Lord, puts the sovereignty of God over all the saint's career..."[7]

There are a few aspects of this patience we can explore. Firstly, patience with regard to our relationship with God.

Patience in Relation to God

Superficially we would think it odd that we should think of being patient with God. But if we are honest, there are times (and for many, this is often) when we lose our patience with God. The road to heaven has many evidences of human footprints that disappear suddenly when those to whom the footprints belong left impatiently.

John Duckworth's book *Joan 'n' the Whale: And Other Stories You Never Heard in Sunday School* is a wonderful collection of thought-provoking stories. One of the stories is "The Man Who Built His House Upon the Rock." It wrote about a man who built his house upon a rock and congratulated himself for being wise. He waited for the rain, knowing that his neighbour's house that was built on sand would collapse. He waited for the storm warnings but they never came. Puzzled, he nevertheless still waited for the storm. He eagerly waited to see the neighbour's house fall, and for his neighbour to beg for shelter in his house. With such smug thoughts he waited for the storm. One day, he heard sounds of yelling and pounding and excitedly told himself that the day had come, only to be disappointed when he looked out of the window. His neighbour was upgrading and converting his house to a beach front resort.

The rains did come one day — but fell only on the house that was built on the rock! The man moaned with dismay and busied himself patching the roof, cleaning the gutters, and bailing out the basement. This went on for quite a while. All this time, the neighbour who built his house on the sand got wealthier, more successful and happier. But the man living in the house on the rock was kept busy coping with a record rainfall that fell only on his house!

Finally the man gave up, saying "Any fool can see that there's not going to be any storm." He packed up his belongings, moved out of his house, and went next door to the luxury beachfront resort. He said, "If you can't beat 'em, join 'em."

"That night, of course, the rain descended, and the floods came, and the winds blew and beat upon both those houses. The one that was built upon the sand fell, and great was the fall of it.

The other fell not; for it was founded upon a rock.

Too bad nobody was home."[8]

The problem highlighted in this story is not with the house on the rock but with the attitude of its inhabitant. He loses patience when he sees that God seems to have forgotten what He had said, and finally abandons the house. There are many who, when they feel that God is too slow or absent, leave through the backdoor and head for the more alluring world.

There are three issues here we must understand.

Firstly, ***God's Perspective***. God has a view of time and history that is different from ours. We are travellers on the road with a limited perspective. We can see only our own current stretches of road, whereas God can see the entire journey and the whole picture. To God, our 1,000 years are like a day (and vice versa) — a truth that reminds us that God has His own sense of timing and timeliness (2 Peter 3:8). We fail to understand this and keep asking, like the little child in the car on a cross-country drive, "How long more?" or "When do we arrive?"

Secondly, ***God's Purpose***. We often expect God to act according to our agenda and wishes. But God is not at our beck and call, serving us to keep us comfortable, prosperous and safe. Our prayers are answered by God only if they are in line with God's will and purposes (1 John 5:14). If God seems to be silent or slow to respond to our urgent prayers, could it be that we have not shifted from our agenda to God's agenda? God's purpose is not to give us a comfortable ride to heaven, but to make us fit for heaven while we are on our way there. If our objectives are mistaken, it is clear that we will lose patience with God, whose objectives are different.

Thirdly, ***God's Presence***. We can be so obsessed with getting experiences and reaching our destination that we may forget that an important part of the journey is to learn to enjoy the delight of God's company. We are focused on results more than the relationship, so much so that we lose our patience when God appears to be slow or silent. We press our spiritual remote controls and feel frustrated that they don't seem to respond to us the way our physical remote controls do. Often nothing happens. Sometimes, there is delayed response. Task-oriented people and Type A personalities will find this most frustrating. They need to learn that we have been created to "glorify God and enjoy Him forever" (Shorter Westminster Catechism).

How then can we learn to be patient with God and in our circumstances? We need to learn how to enjoy God's presence along the way. Often, like the world around us, we are rushing around wanting this or that; we grow impatient with each passing year. And all the time, God wants us to slow down and linger in His presence rather than impatiently rush from one task to another, and from one programme to another.

We must also learn to trust God — and His perspective and purposes. If He has promised something, He will carry it out, in His own timing. Though the Lord has promised He would return, He has not done so yet, and 2000 years have gone by. Should we impatiently ignore His promise or modify our understanding that He was only referring to it in a metaphorical and symbolic sense? Scripture tells us that if there is a "delay" in Christ's return, it is not because God is "slow in keeping his promise, as some understand slowness" but that He is exercising patience, "not wanting anyone to perish but everyone to come to repentance" (2 Peter 3:9).

God showed that He can wait, as when He "waited patiently" for old Noah to build the ark (1 Peter 3:20). In our grossly limited vision, God may appear slow, but in His own eyes, God keeps perfect timing. God will definitely keep all His promises. We are told that He is working all things for our good (Romans 8:28) and this will become perfectly clear one day when we will marvel at both His faithfulness and sense of timing.

Because of God's perspective and purpose, suffering would most likely be part and parcel of our life in Christ. The purpose of our sufferings is our transformation — till Christ is formed in us (Galatians 4:19). It is when we go through such suffering that we are challenged to exercise patience as we wait for God and trust Him for everything, the way Jesus did on His way to the cross. The servants of Christ have done the same (2 Corinthians 6:6). The Holy Spirit will give us His power so that we may have "great endurance and patience" in our sufferings and trials (Colossians 1:11). We are called to be Spirit-filled Christians, "joyful in hope, patient in affliction, faithful in prayer." Hope, joy, patience, faithfulness and prayer are all essential ingredients of the Christian's response in affliction.

Patience in Relation to Others

Research shows, and our own experience and reflection would tell us, that we tend to be more patient with ourselves than with others. Part of it is due to our own blind spots, part of it is due to our self-love. As children of God, however, we are called to "be patient with everyone" (1 Thessalonians 5:14) — and this means all who are around us, without exception. Christian patience is particularly required in two general situations.

Patience when Others are Slow

A boy realised that God had made him fast. He wanted to have a race in his village to prove his speed. People from his village and all the surrounding villages were invited, either as competitors or spectators. When the day of the race came, a wise man came from another village to observe the race, which the boy won easily. He was elated and everyone congratulated him. Some months later he wanted another race, and a wider net was cast to invite more people. Again the boy won the race and was congratulated by the crowd.

The wise man then organised a third race for the boy. This time, the boy had two competitors, a blind man and an old lady. When the whistle was blown to start the race, the boy started off and ran the race with the speed that became his trademark. But to his disappointment, he noticed after winning the race that he had run alone. His competitors were hardly off the starting point. There was no applause this time from the embarrassed crowd. The boy then asked the wise man why the applause was not like before. The wise man told the boy to run the race again, but this time, he instructed him to hold the hands of the blind man and the old lady and to walk with them to the finish line. He did so, and when he passed the line, there was a huge applause from the crowd. The wise man then told the boy, "Your victory today is bigger than all your previous victories. Learn from this." The boy had to learn that it was service rather than speed that mattered in the race of life.[9]

We live in an impatient world and are surrounded by impatient people. Our highways, airports, restaurants, shopping centres, schools and hospitals are places where impatience seems to breed. Our rat race remains one because those who are in front tend to neglect those who are behind. Some people are slow by nature or by circumstances. Impatient people need to appreciate them and show them respect and kindness. The problem with impatience is that we are all rushing somewhere elusive and ignore or ill-treat the people around us because of our impatience and short fuses.

Patience when Others are Sinful

It is not easy to be patient when someone does something bad to you. Perhaps the first time, you can let him off. But what if he repeats it? This was a question Peter asked Jesus; Peter even offered a possible answer — seven times? — to make it easier for Jesus. Perhaps he wanted Jesus to say, "Yes, that's the limit." But Jesus said "seventy-times-seven" which does not mean 490 times (for it was not an arithmetic problem) but "all the time."

Jesus further explained His answer with a parable. A man owed his master a huge sum of money which he was never going to be able to repay. The consequence was that he and his family were to be sold as slaves. The man begged for mercy and the kind master forgave him his debt. But this servant met another servant who owed a small sum of money (a very tiny amount compared to his own debt that was cancelled). The other servant begged this ungrateful servant but received no mercy. He was thrown into a debtors' prison. When the master heard about this, he became angry and asked the foolish and ungrateful servant, "Shouldn't you have had mercy on your fellow servant just as I had on you?" The master threw the servant into jail.

The point Jesus was making is this: How can we fail to be patient with someone else when God has been and continues to be patient with us? We must keep standing at the cross and living at its foot to understand this. We are called to be "completely humble and gentle", patient and "bearing with one another in love" (Ephesians 4:1-2). This is possible only when we are near the cross (where we are reminded of our own great indebtedness to our merciful God).

Dietrich Bonhoeffer shares how praying for those who hurt or oppose us can free us to love them and be patient with them:

> "I can no longer condemn or hate a brother for whom I pray, no matter how much trouble he causes me. His face, hitherto may have been strange and intolerable to me, is transformed in intercession into a countenance of a brother for whom Christ died, the face of a forgiven sinner. This is a happy discovery for the Christian who begins to pray for others. There is no dislike, no personal tension, no estrangement that cannot be overcome by intercession as far as our side is concerned. How does this happen? Intercession means no more than to bring our brother into the presence of God, to see him under the Cross of Jesus as a poor human being and sinner in need of grace. Then everything in him that repels us falls away; we see him in all his destitution and need. His need and his sin become so heavy and oppressive that we feel them as our own, and we can do nothing else but pray...To make intercession means to grant our brother the same right that we have received, namely to stand before Christ and share his mercy."[10]

Henri Nouwen spent his last decade serving at a facility for adults who suffered from severe intellectual disabilities. Nouwen, who was a famous academic and writer, served as the chaplain. Though it was not required of him, Nouwen decided to take care of a man called Adam every morning. Adam was like an infant, unable to take care of himself. Every day he had to be washed, shaved, fed and dressed. When asked why he needed to do this, Nouwen shared the liturgical value of his caregiving ritual. For him, as he took care of the drooling uncoordinated Adam every day, he was reminded of how God was similarly, in a spiritual way, taking care of him patiently. As Paul reminds us, love is always patient (1 Corinthians 13:4).[11]

The Spirit Works Slowly

Today we live with a production mindset. Robots produce our cars in factory lines. Fewer and fewer things are made carefully by skilled craftsmen. No wonder that things don't last long these days; perhaps they are designed that way.

The Bible speaks of spiritual growth more in terms of agricultural metaphors. The sheep that the shepherd takes care of are living animals that take time to grow up; they have to be fed and protected. The tree takes time to grow while it is tended to carefully. The vine has to be pruned. All this means that the farmer cannot afford to be impatient. Fruit is the result of patient hard work.

We need to remember this when we think of our spiritual growth and of the sacred task of making disciples. We cannot mass-produce disciples. Disciples, in the biblical way, are apprentices. They are ultimately apprenticed to Jesus, and this is achieved often through one-to-one mentoring. Mentoring is like parenting; it requires much patience. There is no overnight magical sprouting of our children. It takes years for them to blossom and mature. Likewise spiritual cultivation and growth takes time.

It is possible to have a factory production mindset when we think of the Holy Spirit. In our workplaces we have short-term KPIs (key performance indicators) — which are often related to what can be measured superficially. The Holy Spirit, on the other hand, deals with lasting fruit. He will take His time, showing the same patience we see in the Father and the Son. It is not that you can decide that Jesus is too "slow" for you and then turn to the Spirit for more thrilling rides. It does not work that way. All the Persons of the Trinity work with the same purpose and patience — they walk and work at the same speed.

This means that as we submit to the ways of God and trust God no matter what the circumstances are, yielding our will to His, then we will experience the fullness of the Spirit. One of the visible effects of this will be growing patience in an impatient world. We will stand out in our attitudes and reactions. We will stand out as God's people clothed in God's patience (Colossians 3:12).

Questions for Reflection

1. Define patience using the word studies offered in this chapter. In what way is God patient with us? How was His patience tested by His people?

2. Jesus is singled out in Scripture for His "immense patience" (1 Timothy 1:16). How did Jesus display patience with His friends and enemies? What lessons can you learn from Him?

3. In what ways are we expected to be patient with God? Why do people become impatient with God? How can we deepen our understanding of the ways of God so that we can learn to be patient in all situations? Do you agree that the Holy Spirit tends to work more slowly than we expect?

4. How can we exercise patience with those who are too slow for us? What about those who fail us or sin against us? Why is such patience necessary for us to grow in grace?

8

KINDNESS: LOVE IN ACTION

At different points in our lives, most of us would have been at the receiving end of a kind act — by a parent, friend, teacher, even a stranger. We know how it feels when we are shown kindness, as when an encouraging word is given, help is offered, or an unexpected and thoughtful act surprises us. Kindness is a wonderful thing. It is love in action.

The Greek word used by Paul in his Galatian list is *chrēstotēs* which refers to kindness and goodness and is often used in reference to God. The Bible describes God as kind and portrays Him as One who acts out His love in kind deeds. The Old Testament Hebrew word which conveys the idea of kindness is the richly wonderful word *hesed*. This word is often used to characterise God's relationship with us. It means love, covenantal faithfulness, loyalty, mercy and kindness. It helps us to note the close and essential connection between love and kindness. The distinctive feature about the kindness that is the fruit of the Spirit is that it arises from divine love. It is love that acts specifically and compassionately to meet the needs of others.

The Kindness of Jesus

God's kindness comes to us especially through Jesus: "And God raised us up with Christ and seated us with him in the heavenly realms in Christ Jesus, in order that in the coming ages he might show the incomparable riches of his grace, *expressed in his kindness to us in Christ Jesus*" (Ephesians 2:6-7, emphasis added). The people who lived during the time of Jesus and had the privilege of meeting Him had the joy of receiving the kindness of God — when Jesus fed the hungry, healed the sick, freed the demonised, taught the ignorant, brought light to the confused, and welcomed little children. From His mouth came "gracious words" — which can also be translated as "kind words" (Luke 4:22).

Reflecting God's Kindness

The kindness of God is depicted in many places in the Old Testament — beginning with the early stories in the Bible. When Adam and Eve had sinned against God and brought great grief and disappointment to God, He nevertheless clothed them with garments of skin (Genesis 3:19). This was a gracious act of kindness, the full significance of which would be known in the sacrifice of the Lamb of God for the atonement of our sins.

God's kindness was shown especially in those moments when human sinfulness and weakness manifested. This was because God acted in mercy and grace, from which come forth His kindness. So, after Cain killed his brother Abel out of intense envy, God allowed Cain to experience the guilt of his heinous sin — continuing guilt, a land that would not cooperate, and the life of a wanderer. Nevertheless, God showed His kindness to Cain when He put a mark on Cain "so that no one who found him would kill him" (Genesis 4:15).

Joseph in the Old Testament suffered unkindness in the hands of his treacherous and jealous brothers but he constantly received the kindness of God, who was with Him through the ups and downs of life. Later Joseph was reconciled with his brothers and reunited with his father Jacob, all of whom benefitted from the kindness of Joseph who was by then second in importance to the Pharaoh in Egypt. Joseph had personally experienced God's kindness all through his years and therefore responded to his brothers with kindness in spite of what they had done to him. He told his brothers, "You intended to harm me, but God intended it for good to accomplish what is now being done, the saving of many lives" (Genesis 50:20). God's kindness stands out amid the unkindness of Joseph's brothers.

Again and again, God treated His people with rich kindness — in the way He delivered them from slavery in Egypt, provided food and water for them as they travelled through the wilderness (often with stubborn rebelliousness), brought them to the promised land, and blessed their land. But God's kindness cannot be taken for granted. He cannot be taken for a ride. We are told that God is both kind and stern (Romans 11:22). Therefore, the Israelites had to face the consequences of their sins, but even in their punishment, God extended mercy and kindness.

After the exile in Babylon, God showed kindness by bringing His people back to the promised land. There in a worship service, the Levites led in a lengthy prayer of confession (Nehemiah 9). In that prayer, there is a litany that narrates the sinful behaviour of the Israelites throughout their history and the gracious responses of God. The prayer is punctuated by a series of "But they"s and "But You"s, one alternating with the other. Every "But they" told the story of Israel's sinful deeds and their ungrateful forgetfulness. Every "But you" told the story of God's forgiveness and kindness, of how each time He heard their cries in the eleventh hour and responded with covenantal love and kindness:

> "*But they* and our fathers acted proudly,
> Hardened their necks,
> And did not heed Your commandments...
> *But You* are God,
> Ready to pardon,
> Gracious and merciful,
> Slow to anger,
> *Abundant in kindness*,
> And did not forsake them" (Nehemiah 9:16-17, NKJV, emphasis added)

God appealed to His sinful people to return to Him because He is of "great kindness" (Joel 2:13). He promised them, "with everlasting kindness I will have compassion on you" (Isaiah 54:8). God's people did not deserve God and the blessings He brought, but God was overflowing with kindness.

Jesus was Kind to All

In Jesus, God's kindness comes to His people in a new way and overflows to the whole world. God expresses His kindness to us in Jesus Christ (Ephesians 2:6-7). When Jesus appeared, "the kindness and love of God our Savior appeared" to save us from our sins (Titus 3:4-8). At the cross of Jesus, the kindness of God continues to flow out to touch the lost world. Those who experience and understand the kindness of God can never be the same again.

The life and ministry of Jesus demonstrated His kindness to people of all walks of life. When He saw the needy crowds pressing into His time and energy, instead of feeling irritated, Jesus felt a deep compassion that moved Him to respond to people with many kind deeds because He saw them as a people who were harassed, helpless and clueless (Matthew 9:36). Not only did Jesus treat the crowds kindly by teaching them and healing the sick, but He also showed the same kindness especially to individuals who sought Him and to those He found languishing in the highways and byways of life. Different individuals experienced firsthand the kindness of Jesus — from the courtly Nicodemus (John 3) to socially ashamed individuals such as Zacchaeus (Luke 19:1-10) and the Samaritan woman of Sychar (John 4), to individuals living in lonely misery and incurable illnesses such as blind Bartimaeus (Mark 10:46-52).

Jesus was Kind to His Disciples

Jesus extended kindness to the needy crowds and individuals. He was also kind to His disciples. At one time, there was so much to do, with the crowds pressing in from all sides, that Jesus and His disciples had no opportunity to eat. Jesus was concerned for His hungry and overworked disciples and wanted them to have a much-needed break. With much kindness, He invited them, "Come with me by yourselves to a quiet place and get some rest" (Mark 6:31).

After He rose from the dead, Jesus met His disciples at the shore of the Sea of Galilee. They had gone fishing the whole night but had caught nothing. They were hungry, tired and frustrated. Jesus spoke to them and gave them instructions on where they should throw their nets, and they caught a huge number of fish. And when they came ashore, Jesus had already prepared breakfast for them. Not having a house of His own, Jesus had turned the shore of the lake into a kitchen and dining room. He did not just tell the disciples to help themselves, but actually *served* them — He "*took* the bread and *gave* it to them, and did the same with the fish" (John 21:12-13, emphasis added). What a thoughtful, touching and kind act!

Jesus was Kind to His Enemies

Jesus showed kindness to His enemies too. Judas Iscariot was a traitor and a thief and found his way into the circle of disciples. Jesus knew what he was up to but nevertheless kept him in the group. He even washed the dirty feet of this treacherous man — an act of genuine kindness. Here Jesus practised what He preached, that we should love our enemies, and that we should emulate God who shows His kindness to both the good and the wicked. At the cross, Jesus extended His kindness by offering the repentant thief hope of a glorious future and a place in His kingdom. He prayed for His enemies and tormentors, asking the Father to forgive them.

Jesus not only showed deep kindness to people, but He also taught much about kindness. He told His listeners about God who gave sunshine to both the evil and the good, and sent rain on both the righteous and the unrighteous (Matthew 5:45). God had amazing kindness — broad and deep.

Jesus Taught about Kindness

Jesus told the famous parable of the Good Samaritan in answer to the question, "Who is my neighbour?" (Luke 10:25-37). The story shows us that kindness is to be expected of us in our everyday routines and that at times religious pursuits and religiosity (of the unhelpful kind) can hinder us from being genuinely kind to those in need. The priest and the Levite both saw the wounded man on the road but "passed by on the other side." There was not even a word of encouragement for the thirsty, hurting and dying man. These were religious professionals, whose job it was to bring people to God and God to people. They were trained in religious language and ritual and were supposed to be full of God's words. Yet, they did not even offer a word, let alone a cup of water and human kindness.

Then came a Samaritan, a member of a highly despised group (as far as the Jews were concerned). The Jewish listeners of Jesus would have thought, "Here is where the story will get from bad to worse!" But Jesus surprised them by telling them how the Samaritan was a truly kind man — a true neighbour. The Samaritan saw the wounded man and, unlike the priest and Levite, "took pity on him." His kindness flowed out of his compassion for the helpless victim.

Why did the Samaritan act in this way, in contrast to the religious professionals? It surely cannot be that he was an idle traveller with lots of time on his hands. He must have been as busy — if not busier — than the priest and Levite. The details of the parable suggest that he was a frequent traveller in that area — he seems to be familiar with the innkeeper. That particular road was a dangerous road, full of robbers. Chances are that the Samaritan himself could have been a victim of robbery at some point in the past. Who knows, he could have had been a victim several times. If he had personal experience of having been a victim on that road, we can understand the depth of his compassion and empathy when he came across another victim on the road.

Kind people have empathy for the needy and broken, and this empathy is deepened by personal suffering. One who had known poverty in childhood will probably better understand the dire straits of a poor child in school. People who are only interested in selfish pursuits and personal comfort, and people who have it good would have to work much harder in feeling compassion and showing kindness. "Sympathy becomes hollow when one does not feel pain."[1] Perhaps, that is why God allows suffering to come to His children — to make us more Christlike, and this includes becoming kinder. When we suffer we have a better chance of experiencing God's kindness. And when others around us suffer, we can show that same kindness that we had received from God (cf. 2 Corinthians 1:3-4).

The good Samaritan went to the victim, poured oil and wine on the man's wounds (as medical treatment) and bandaged them. He seemed to have had a mobile "first-aid kit." He seemed prepared to show kindness whenever it was needed. He was a man ready to be kind. A similar attitude today would be when we visit a relatively poor country — as we leave the hotel or house, we could put some money in our pockets or useful foodstuff in our bags to be given away to needy people we will meet along the way. Readiness to be kind — that's a wonderful spiritual discipline we could all practise as children of God who receive God's kindness every day.

Second-Mile Kindness

Jesus taught about godly kindness that is quite unique. People do kind deeds for all kinds of reasons. One may show kindness to another hoping that the kind act would be reciprocated in some way. Or one may show kindness simply out of necessity or duty. Such kind acts are kind only on the surface — they are superficial acts. Other acts are done for show and for personal glory, the way that the rich gave money in the temple, throwing their coins into the noisy metal offering containers.

The kindness Jesus taught is the kind that goes the second mile: "If someone forces you to go one mile, go with him two miles" (Matthew 5:41). The Roman soldiers who occupied the land of Jesus had the official authority to make anyone carry a load for them — and the legal maximum distance was a mile. Jews who found themselves doing such "national service" would mutter under their breath and do what they were forced to do grudgingly. Jesus challenged His listeners to surprise the Romans by going an extra mile. Would not that act of kindness touch some Roman soldier and make him think more deeply about the faith of the Jews? Christian kindness goes beyond a sense of obligation and duty. It comes from a sincere heart that is truly kind, and does not expect anything in return.

Practising Kindness

Every day we have opportunities to practise kindness, to show some kindness to the different people we come across. Kind acts are not limited by a list of things we can do. They are as broad as life is broad and can be as creative as human needs are varied. It may be in the form of an encouraging word, a helping hand, a listening ear, being quietly present in a hospital room, sharing a meal, a timely letter of introduction, and a host of other things.

Sociologist Robert Wuthnow has shown in his study of young volunteers involved in serving their community that performing acts of caring is more learned than innate.[2] Kindness can be learned and nurtured, and one of the best places this can take place is the religious environment — whether at home or in church. This has implications for what we do in the family and in church. How we can teach and model kindness, and how people can learn to be kind are questions that need to be thought through carefully, especially as we live in a modern society where the pursuits of the self have meant that the needs of others tend to be overlooked and where coarseness of culture is fast replacing kindness in society.

Elisabeth Elliot's prayer is a thought-provoking and challenging call to practice kindness in all kinds of ways, and to root our acts of kindness in our relationship with Jesus:

> "Lord, break the chains that hold me to myself; free me to be Your happy slave — that is, to be the happy foot washer of anyone today who needs his feet washed, his supper cooked, his faults overlooked, his work commended, his failure forgiven, his griefs consoled or his button sewed on. Let me not imagine that my love for You is very great if I am unwilling to do for a human being something very small."[3]

Our claim to love God must be proven by our acts of kindness done to others in the course of our daily routines, a point reiterated by the apostle John (1 John 4:20) and others in Scripture.

Can We Be Kind to God?

Someone asked about showing kindness to God. Should we be kind to God? Does God need our kindness? God has no needs. While we are to love Him with all our hearts, He does not need our kindness. Our love is expressed through our worship of Him and our obedience to Him. But He does not need our kindness.

In another sense, though, we can show kindness to God. Jesus put it this way: "For I was hungry and you gave me something to eat, I was thirsty and you gave me something to drink, I was a stranger and you invited me in, I needed clothes and you clothed me, I was sick and you looked after me, I was in prison and you came to visit me…*whatever you did for one of the least of these brothers of mine, you did for me*" (Matthew 25:35-36, 40, emphasis added).

There is a profound spirituality about being kind here. What we do to the often neglected and ignored "least of these" is like doing it to Jesus. Mother Teresa saw Jesus in the faces of the poor and dying sick that she ministered to in the streets of Calcutta, and showed her love for Him by showing her love for these poor people. When asked how many times a day she met Jesus, she replied that she met Jesus once in her morning devotions, and then for the rest of the day in the faces of the needy people she served. In showing kindness to them, she showed kindness to Jesus.

If we consider the way Matthew lays out the teaching of Jesus concerning the final judgment, we will not be judged in terms of all the spectacular religious things we have done for God such as prophesying, casting out demons or performing miracles (Matthew 7:21-23), but in terms of the little acts of kindness we do when we come across the poor and needy (Matthew 25:31-46). This is important to bear in mind for we surely do not want to be like the student who studied the wrong chapters for his exam.

But pleasing God is not just about passing the exam, and the final judgment is not quite like mugging up for an exam. The reason why Jesus described His judgment in the terms mentioned in Matthew 7 and 25 is that we will be judged according to the kind of people we have been and become. The evidence that we have placed faith in Christ and have received the new life is that we will be dwelling in

Christ and be filled with the Spirit. We will then bear spiritual fruit. The fruit will show what sort of tree it is. And one key fruit of the Spirit is kindness, which will be to God, an indicator of whether we have truly believed, and whether we have been saved and have the life of Jesus in us. This is how we will be judged.

Walk with Kindness

In modern busyness it is easy to run the rat race without any time or care to show kindness to those we pass by. While the "sheep" in Matthew 25 were commended for the kind acts they did, the "goats" were admonished for the kind acts they failed to do.

> "It isn't the thing you do, dear,
> It's the thing you leave undone,
> Which gives you the bitter heartache
> At the setting of the sun;
> The tender word unspoken,
> The letter you did not write,
> The flower you might have sent, dear,
> Are your haunting ghosts at night.
>
> The stone you might have lifted
> Out of your brother's way,
> The bit of heartsome counsel
> You were hurried too much to say;
> The loving touch of the hand, dear,
> The gentle and winsome tone,
> That you had no time or thought for,
> With troubles enough of your own.
>
> These little acts of kindness,
> So easily out of mind,
> These chances to be angels,
> Which even mortals find
> They come in night and silence,
> Each chill reproachful wraith,

When hope is faint and flagging,
And a blight has dropped on faith.

For life is all too short, dear.
And sorrow is all too great,
To suffer our slow compassion
That tarries until too late.
And it's not the thing you do, dear,
It's the thing you leave undone,
Which gives you the bitter heartache,
At the setting of the sun."[4]

Adelaide Proctor's (1825-1864) poem expresses the danger of walking through our days without kindness because we are too busy pursuing self-serving personal ambitions or too slow in responding compassionately. The key is to walk kindly by walking with the Lord who loves us with everlasting kindness.

Questions for Reflection

1. God has "great kindness" (Joel 2:13). How has God shown His kindness to His people and the world? How has God shown kindness to you?

2. What can we learn about kindness from Jesus? What did He teach about kindness? How practical is second-mile kindness? How did Jesus practice what He taught?

3. In what way can we be kind to God? Why is showing kindness to a stranger and the last, least, and the lost like showing kindness to God? How is this important on the Day of judgment (Matthew 25:31-46)?

4. In what way is kindness the result of the work of the Spirit? How can we cooperate with the Spirit in practising kindness and cultivating it as a virtue? How would kindness look like in your life and its many relationships?

9

GOODNESS: THE INTEGRITY OF LOVE

A class of primary school students was asked what they would like to be when they grew up. We know what the usual answers may be, but what was surprising was that a significant number of responses were along the lines of "I would like to be rich." Ask any parent what they would like their children to grow up to be and they would give various answers, usually having to do with nice jobs and the like. Thankfully, a few would say that they would like their children to be good. Is that not one of the noblest and most important of aspirations?

When we say that so-and-so is a good man, we can mean several things. We can mean that he is a kind man — kindness and goodness have a lot in common (and also common connotations in the Bible). We can also mean that the man is an upright man — someone with integrity.

The original Greek word in Paul's list in Galatians is *agathōsunē*. The word indicates "that quality in a man who is ruled by and aims at what is good, namely, the quality of moral worth."[1] Besides referring to moral goodness and soundness, the word also refers to wholeness or wholesomeness. A related word is *kalos* which connotes beauty, rightness and virtue.

Are Human Beings Good?

A rich young ruler came to Jesus with the question, "What must I do to get eternal life?" Jesus replied, "Why do you ask me what is good?" He explained further by declaring, "There is only One who is good, If you want to enter life, obey the commandments" (Matthew 19:16-17). In saying this, Jesus was telling the young man that the reference point for goodness is God Himself, for He is the source of all goodness. If we want to know about goodness we must turn to God. Humanistic goodness focuses on doing good acts. It has some underlying principles such as human rights, equality and freedom. But the values and principles of humanism have become delinked with original Christian principles, and now have taken on distorted expressions.

In addition, the good things that human beings do without any reference to God often end up in self-interest. One may volunteer for a worthy cause for a selfish reason — for human praise, social standing or some other personal gain. One may give a donation just to get the person collecting donations off his back.

In the ultimate sense God is the only Good One. If we are capable of showing goodness, it is only because we are strengthened by Him or that we have some bits of goodness left from what He created us with. After God created everything, including human beings, He "saw all that he had made, and it was very good" (Genesis 1:31). But sin has distorted and marred everything. After God had made man good, man wanted to be good in his own ways, out of self-centred ambition and without reference to God — he wanted to be his own god. Man lost his innocence and goodness and everything was tainted by sinfulness. It was so bad that the Bible describes the depth of depravity in the human heart in this way: "every inclination of the thoughts of his heart was only evil all the time" (Genesis 6:5). The psalmist echoes this observation when he laments, "there is no one who does good, not even one" (Psalm 14:3, 1). Man is not only not good but he has a poverty of good deeds.

Human goodness is not a stable standard as we have been tainted by sin. Even our best efforts are often darkened by some sinful motive or less than noble intention. If we all have watches that are faulty in some way, no one can tell for sure what the actual time is. We can fix our times to one of the watches, but we would be still off the mark.

For us to know the actual time we have to find a watch that is totally reliable and can tell us the time accurately.

Likewise, for our understanding of goodness we must turn to God who alone is truly good (Psalm 86:5). That is why Jesus turned the young man's attention to God — away from social standards or the standards of his own sinful heart.

God's Goodness

A W Tozer writes of God's goodness in this way and points out why it is important to hold on to the truth of God's goodness:

> "The goodness of God is that which disposes Him to be kind, cordial, benevolent, and full of good will toward men. He is tenderhearted and of quick sympathy, and His unfailing attitude toward all moral beings is open, frank, and friendly. By His nature, He is inclined to bestow blessedness and He takes holy pleasure in the happiness of His people... To allow that God could be other than good is to deny the validity of all thought and end in the negation of every moral judgment. If God is not good, then there can be no distinction between kindness and cruelty, and heaven can be hell and hell, heaven."[2]

God is the standard and source of all goodness. He is not only perfectly good in what He is, but also in what He does. "You are good, and what you do is good; teach me your decrees" (Psalm 119:68). It is because we learn goodness from God that we must give special attention to His laws and commandments because they have to do with goodness. Jesus, therefore, told the rich young ruler that if he was thinking of what good he must do to gain eternal life, he must turn to God and His commandments — he must obey them (Matthew 19:17). The psalmist goes the same way in that after declaring God to be good in who He is and what He does, he prays to God to teach him His laws (Psalm 119:68).

In His conversation with the rich young man, Jesus mentioned the details of the Decalogue (Ten Commandments) when the man asked Jesus to specify the commandments he had in mind. The young man declared that he had kept all the commandments mentioned by Jesus but still felt that something was lacking. He was a good man by most standards, and yet he felt that his goodness was not enough to gain eternal life. Therefore he asked Jesus (obviously with some degree of sincere desperation), "What do I still lack?" (Matthew 19:20).

The answer that Jesus gave teaches us some important truths about divine goodness. The Ten Commandments, which are mostly phrased in terms of prohibitions, should not be misinterpreted as only a list of "Do not's." Goodness is not just avoiding sin, but actively showing love. It is not just the absence of sin but is also the presence of love and mercy. Thus, Jesus told the young man to "go sell your possessions and give to the poor...Then come follow me" (Matthew 19:21). There are five verbs in the instructions of Jesus: Go, Sell, Give, Come, Follow. Each of these had to do with faith and obedience. Each of this had to do with true goodness, the goodness of God. Tragically, the young man loved his wealth too much and was unable to follow Jesus and pursue divine goodness.

In our own strength and using our own devices we cannot do good God's way. Doing good deeds must arise from being good, and that is where we have a serious problem because of the inherent sinfulness that is lodged deeply in us. The only way we can be good is to repent and turn to Christ and have His Spirit dwell in us following our regeneration. That is how it is possible. As Jesus said, "With man this is impossible, but with God all things are possible (Matthew 19:26). Then we can truly follow Jesus and as the Spirit empowers us, we can live like Jesus lived.

The Goodness of Jesus

The psalmist challenges us to "Taste and see that the Lord is good" (Psalm 34:8). The people who met Jesus during His time on earth had the opportunity to see the goodness of God perfectly demonstrated in Jesus. The goodness of God appeared perfectly in Jesus (Titus 3:4, ESV). Just as God made all His goodness to pass before the eager Moses who wanted to see God (Exodus 33:19), so He did the same when Jesus walked on earth. In Jesus we see all the goodness of God.

There was No Sin in Jesus

The people around Jesus saw in Him the holiness of God, so much so that the early church declared what the witnesses had declared — that Jesus was sinless. Peter wrote that "He committed no sin" (1 Peter 2:22) while John testified that "in him is no sin" (1 John 3:5). The writer of Hebrews says that Jesus was "tempted in every way, just as we are — yet was without sin" (Hebrews 4:15). Paul, too, emphasised that Jesus "had no sin" (2 Corinthians 5:21). The consistent and overwhelming unanimity of the witnesses who encountered Jesus is that He was morally perfect — as good as God is good. Scripture also tells us that this was so because Jesus Himself is God.

Even ungodly people noted that Jesus was uniquely sinless and faultless. The political and cowardly Pontius Pilate, after trying Jesus in his court, concluded that he could not find any fault with Jesus (Luke 23:4, 14). One of the thieves hanging on the cross next to Jesus testified that Jesus "has done nothing wrong" (Luke 23:41) and was so taken by the goodness of Jesus that in his dying moments, he believed in Jesus and placed his trust in Him.

Jesus was Wholesomely Good

Jesus showed goodness not only in what He did not do (commit sins) but in also who He was and what He did. There was a godly innocence about Him. He was transparently good, one who had absolute integrity, and was filled with goodness like no other. Women could talk to him and touch him without fear of being taken advantage of. Children could come to Him and be lifted to His shoulders without being abused as if they were less than human. Lepers could approach Him and receive kindness. The desperate cries of a blind man who was ignored by the passing crowds was heard by Jesus, who helped the man. Self-righteous men were silenced by the holy eyes with which He looked at them when they brought sinners to be judged by Him. Jesus exuded goodness that could not be ignored, that caused joy and also trepidation. In Jesus we see the beauty of God's character; goodness goes together with spiritual and moral beauty. As it is said of God, "great is his goodness, and how great his beauty!" (Zechariah 9:17, ESV). The same is true of Jesus the Son of God.

Jesus did Good Things to People

Jesus was the good shepherd who laid down His life for His sheep (John 10:11). He touched people's lives with His goodness, bringing light where there was darkness, healing where there was illness, strength where there was weakness, hope where there was despair, clarity where there was confusion, faith where there was doubt, purity where there was sin, and love where there was hatred or indifference. Jesus even healed people and delivered them from their misery on the Sabbath day. When challenged by the narrow-minded and blinded religious leaders, Jesus proclaimed that "it is lawful to do good on the Sabbath" (Matthew 12:12). Jesus was not against the Sabbath (which was instituted by God) but He was against the man-made rules that were so tightly tied around the Sabbath that they distorted what God had intended. Against their anaemic and soul-diminishing legalism, Jesus connected the Sabbath with practising goodness — as God intended it to be.

In His Teaching, Jesus Emphasised Goodness

In His Sermon on the Mount, Jesus showed how God's children were to live lives of goodness, and how they should treat one another. They should even be good to their enemies, because God Himself shows His goodness (sending rain and sunshine) to both the evil and the good (Matthew 5:43-48). Their lives should be like salt and light in the world in the way they practised goodness, living upright lives and showing compassion. Jesus instructed His listeners, "let your light shine before men, that they may see your good deeds and praise your Father in heaven" (Matthew 5:16). The fruit of goodness in the lives of God's children will bring glory to their heavenly Father.

Jesus also told stories: the Good Samaritan who practised good deeds even as he went about his daily travels, and the Sower and the Seed. In the latter parable, while describing different kinds of soil, Jesus commended the good soil which received the seed of God's Word positively and brought forth much fruit (Mark 4:1-12). God's goodness in the lives of His children is just like that. It is found in the seed that is planted in them. It makes them good and helps them to bear the fruit of goodness.

In the end, the death and resurrection of Jesus confirms God's goodness and its ultimate triumph. We dare not trust our own goodness which is fragile, unreliable and poisoned. But the goodness of God as expressed in Jesus is our guarantee that we will have a future that is good, even as we remember that God created everything for good. Frank White notes:

> "But our faith is not in ourselves, or in our goodness, but in God, the source of all goodness. Genesis tells us that God saw everything that he had made, and behold it was very good. That means that there is a fundamental goodness in creation, so well-rooted that no evil can in the end blot it out; because always, no matter what happens, good will surface once more. And of that truth, the resurrection is the guarantee."[3]

Being Good

We now move to the practice of goodness in our lives. How is goodness — the fruit of the Spirit — manifested in the believers' daily life and practice?

It is useful to remember Psalm 119:68, which the ESV translates as "You are good and do good." Being good and doing good are closely connected. We do good *because* we are good. Jesus said that it is the good tree that will bear good fruit: "No good tree bears bad fruit, nor does a bad tree bear good fruit. Each tree is recognized by its own fruit...The good man brings good things out of the good stored up in his heart, and the evil man brings evil things out of the evil stored up in his heart" (Luke 6:43-45). One can appear to bear good fruit, but the goodness of a fruit is in its taste. Another way of saying that is that goodness is not only assessed in terms of an act but also its motive. Hence, Jesus points to the danger of appearing not to break the Law in an act, while already having broken it in one's own heart (Matthew 5:21-30, in relation to hatred and lust).

It is possible to attempt to do good but if we do not focus on being good, then one of the following may happen.

- ***We become frustrated and discouraged*** that it is not possible to do good as we aspire or hope to do. Paul deals with this frustration when he wrote, "For I have the desire to do what is good, but I cannot carry it out. For what I do is not the good I want" (Romans 7:18-19). This is the frustration of the "wretched man" (Romans 7:24) who wakes up with noble plans in the morning and goes to bed at night knowing that he has failed miserably. He is like a man who dreams of standing on a breathtaking mountain top, but finds himself in a dingy prison.

- ***We become hypocritical.*** We attempt to do good things but we know that we are not really good deep within. What we are does not match what we seem to be doing. Our external conduct does not match our internal character. We go through the motions of doing good, and may even be appreciated by those around us, but we know that it is a sham. But because we know of no other way, we master the art of pretending. The Pharisees were described by Jesus as "whitewashed tombs" who appeared to look good and beautiful but were unclean inside. Jesus told them, "On the outside you appear to people as righteous but on the inside you are full of hypocrisy and wickedness" (Matthew 23:28).

- ***We become self-deceived and superficial.*** Our goodness is only limited to our external conduct, and this is often restricted to religious rituals and superficial habits. By playing church, we may deceive and lull ourselves to sleep, thinking that we are doing well and that we are good in the eyes of God. Jesus told many wonderful and powerful parables. One of them was about two worshippers who went to the temple to pray (Luke 18:9-14). One of them was a Pharisee, a very religious man in the eyes of the others. He was like those who had gathered around Jesus, "who were confident of their own righteousness and looked down on everybody else." The other was a tax-collector; people in his occupation were generally recognised as terrible sinners, traitors to their own people as they worked for the occupying foreign Roman government and made a lot of money in their jobs.

  As Jesus told the story, His listeners would have thought that it was clear which of the two men was good, and which was not good. But Jesus challenged their assumptions. The Pharisee, looking only at his outward and superficial acts of goodness, prayed with pride and about himself. His prayer was one of self-congratulation at how good he was: "God, I thank you that I am not like other people — robbers, evildoers, adulterers — or even like this tax collector. I fast twice a week and give a tenth of all I get." The tax-collector, realising his inner rottenness, pleaded for God's mercy and forgiveness: "God, have mercy on me a sinner." The repentant tax-collector was on his way to becoming good. The Pharisee, tragically, would be trapped in his self-deception and had closed the door to becoming good.

It is important to realise that the path of goodness begins for us when we become good, and we stay on it by remaining good. Regeneration of the sinner by the power of God begins this journey. The power and presence of the indwelling Holy (Good) Spirit will enable us to be filled with the fullness of Jesus. His life will be lived in and through us. We will find goodness surging within us and may even be surprised by how we are able to be and do good.

At the heart of this is surrendering to Jesus and obeying Him wholeheartedly, remaining in Him and growing in His love. Goodness will arise from the reality of this relationship. We do not need to be frustrated, hypocritical, self-deceived or superficial. We can grow tall with the goodness of the Lord. We will reflect His integrity, wholeness, wholesomeness, sincerity, trustworthiness and compassion.

Doing Good

Being good will help us to do good. The life that is lived in Christ will bring forth all kinds of good deeds in our lives — the way Jesus did good in his earthly life and ministry.

Goodness, as expressed in good deeds, is something God has designed for us. "For we are God's workmanship, created to do good works which God prepared in advance for us to do" (Ephesians 2:10). While we are not saved *by* good works (because people are not able to do it) but by God's grace, we are saved *for* good works (because saved people are empowered to do the works that reflect the character of God).

God has revealed the shape of goodness that He expects of us. "He has showed you, O man, what is good. And what does the Lord require of you? To act justly and to love mercy and to walk humbly with your God" (Micah 6:8). Jesus demonstrated this in the goodness He had and in the many good deeds that filled His life and ministry.

Every day we have opportunities to do good like Jesus and to do that in His name. We are called to "abound in every good work" (2 Corinthians 9:8) and to "be rich in good deeds" (1 Timothy 6:18). This is made possible if we learn to seek the good (as in benefits and wellbeing) of others more than our own good (1 Corinthians 10:24).

There are numerous ways in which we can do good. Even in our daily interactions and in places where we least expect, like on the road, whatever good we do can touch the lives of many people.

We must spend all the moments of our days with care, not missing opportunities to do good. "Do not withhold good from those who deserve it, when it is in your power to act" (Proverbs 3:27). We should not postpone to tomorrow the good we can do today, for the opportunity may never come again.

We should seek to remain in Christ and live the Spirit-filled life; then we will be good and become good. In one sense, goodness is an effortless reality. In another sense goodness has to do with active cooperation with God's operations and the practice of spiritual disciplines and habits. This is the paradox of Christian discipleship and the development of Christ's character and virtues — the fruit of the Spirit. It is the paradox of how grace and spiritual discipline work together.

Bearing this in mind, the following can be noted:

- ***Read the Word***. Scripture teaches, rebukes, corrects and trains in righteousness "so that the man of God may be *thoroughly equipped for every good work*" (2 Timothy 3:16-17, emphasis added). The Bible defines godly goodness and helps to shape our moral universe. It will rebuke us when we are hypocritical or lazy, and it will bring us to Jesus and His good ways so that we can spiritually observe the Lord at work and emulate Him through the power of the Holy Spirit.

- ***Pray for people***. A habit of praying for people you meet every day can be used by the Spirit to show us their needs and help us to practise goodness, even to those who are difficult, unlovely or hostile.

- ***Be prepared to do good***. This is both in terms of attitude as well as "equipment." We should wake up in the morning with a resolve to walk with Jesus and to do good as opportunity provides (Galatians 6:10). John Wesley took this seriously and made it into a rule that he followed diligently and encouraged his fellow Methodists to adopt. He wrote, "Do all the good you can. By all the means you can. In all the ways you can. In all the places you can. At all the times you can. To all the people you can. As long as ever you can."[4] The "equipment" refers to things we can carry with us that would help us to do good regularly, even in unexpected moments. These may include some books, brochures or tracts in the car, some loose change and an encouraging thought or saying or Bible passage that we can share with others.

- ***Watch your company***. "Bad company corrupts good character" (1 Corinthians 15:33). The company we keep will affect our character. This does not mean that we should have nothing to do with those who are ungodly. In fact, we should reach out to them, in the same way Jesus related with the sinners and publicans, even though He was severely criticised for it. The point is that Jesus had a positive effect on the sinners and did not allow their sinful habits and ways to corrupt Him. What Paul says in this verse is that we should be careful that evil companions do not change our thinking and ways and rob us of our goodness. In another sense, we should also be careful of what we read, watch and hear. Media content, literature, music and the like can corrupt us. We must watch the inputs, interactions and influences in our lives.

- ***Do not be discouraged***. Being good and doing good may be resisted, laughed at, misunderstood, sidelined or even condemned. Paul encouraged the Galatians to "not become weary in doing good" (Galatians 6:9) and urged others to "cling to what is good" (Romans 12:9) and to "Hold on to the good" (1 Thessalonians 5:21).

- ***Our good deeds will bring others to God***. After urging his readers to "abstain from sinful desires" Peter encourages them, "Live such good lives among the pagans that...they may see your good deeds and glorify God on the day he visits us" (1 Peter 2:11-12). We are challenged to "adorn the doctrine of God" (Titus 2:10, ESV) with good lives and good deeds, so that our teaching and preaching will be made attractive by the godly beauty of our lives.

God is the unique source and standard of all goodness. Because He is good, we His children are also called to be good. This is possible when we turn over our lives to His Son and Spirit. Consider Barnabas (the biblical "son of encouragement") who is described as "a good man, full of the Holy Spirit" (Acts 11:24). In him we see the sure connection between Spirit-fullness and goodness. When the life of Jesus is imparted to us by the Spirit as we surrender to Christ by faith, then not only will we imitate Christ, but we will feel His life flowing in and through us. We will bear His goodness in our thoughts, words, deeds, and daily interactions. Our lives will reflect the beauty of the goodness of God as it follows us all the days of our lives (Psalm 23:6). We will be rich in good deeds and bring glory to God the Father.

Questions for Reflection

1. "God is the source of all goodness." Discuss this statement and share why it is important for us to recognise it. What did Jesus teach about goodness and how did He show it? What lessons can we learn from Him about goodness?

2. Why do modern people focus more on looking good rather than in being good? How can Christians resist such cultural pressures and focus on what is important?

3. Discuss Micah 6:8. What are the implications of this verse on how we conduct our lives, what we focus on, and what motivates us?

4. How can we be more intentional in being good and in doing good? Discuss the practical suggestions in the chapter. Can you add other helpful suggestions to the list?

10

FAITHFULNESS: THE LOYALTY OF LOVE

The original Greek word *pistis* in Paul's list of the fruit of the Holy Spirit means faith and faithfulness. In this instance, it refers to faithfulness, fidelity and loyalty.

Faith and faithfulness are related. One cannot say that he has faith in God if he is also not faithful to God. The two go together, just as they are rooted in the same word.

The Hebrew word in the Old Testament that conveys the same meaning is *emunah.* It means "faithfulness, trustworthiness, integrity" and "occurs in the context of moral language (steadfast love, righteousness, justice, etc.) and is used to reveal God's character, often in language of praise."[1] We note that faithfulness is also connected with truth and truthfulness. It is built on the solid base of integrity.

God is Faithful

Scripture praises God for His absolute faithfulness, which is an integral part of His character. He was introduced to the Israelites as the God who is faithful throughout all generations: "Know therefore that the Lord your God is God; *he is the faithful God*, keeping his covenant of love to a thousand generations of those who love him and keep his commandments" (Deuteronomy 7:9, emphasis added). God is a covenant-making God and His covenants are built on His abiding love and the strength of His word. In His covenantal love and truth, He keeps His every word: "The LORD is faithful in all his words" (Psalm 145:13, ESV).

Even when the people of God proved to be unfaithful, as when they built a golden calf when Moses did not return from Mt Sinai as quickly as they desired, God declared Himself as abundantly faithful. He reassured Moses that He was "abounding in love and faithfulness" (Exodus 34:6; cf. Psalm 86:15). Paul knew this when he argued that God's faithfulness is infinitely more resilient, and will outlast the faithlessness of His people. He asked, "Will their lack of faith nullify God's faithfulness?" and answered with a resounding "Not at all!" (Romans 3:3).

The adage that used to be repeated in church — that even if we let go of Him, God will never let go of us — points to this truth about the marathon faithfulness of God (2 Timothy 2:13). Of course, this should not be an excuse for us to live as we please, but it is a humble expression of our confidence in God's promises and His character that will ensure that He will keep all His promises. Paul again helps us by arguing, "Shall we go on sinning so that grace may increase? By no means!" (Romans 6:1). We should not be presumptuous about God's faithfulness, for He cannot be taken for a ride. But we can always trust His faithfulness when we are weak and faltering, when the going gets tough, or when it appears that He has forgotten us.

According to Katherine Doob Sakenfeld, Paul argued for the untiring and sure faithfulness of God so well that his warning in Romans 6:1 — that we should not take such divine grace for granted does not diminish but enhances his stirring argument in Romans 8:

> "The apostle Paul's ringing assurance in Romans 8 that nothing in all creation can separate us from the love of God in Christ reflects the abounding sure loyalty of God. In the face of persecution and tribulation, peril and sword, Paul comes to know that God's loyalty goes even beyond deliverance from enemies, or constant protection, or bringing the situation right from a human point of view. For loyalty in the end even overcomes death — neither life nor death can separate us

> from the love of God. Thus God's loyalty is not to be measured by one's lot in life; it is promised despite all enemies. But to those who place their trust in God, it is promised as well despite all human failing and backsliding."[2]

What is also truly amazing and countercultural about God's faithfulness and loyalty is that it is directed to those who are subordinate to Him. We normally think of loyalty in terms of being loyal to our superiors, but God shows His loyalty to the poor and the weak, reflecting the amazing ways of His covenant-making and covenant-keeping faithfulness.

The words that were used in the worship of God in Israel praised Him for His faithfulness. They sang to God, "your faithfulness reaches to the skies" (Psalm 57:10), remembering how God had again and again proven His reliability and faithfulness to His people, especially during difficult times. In this particular psalm, there is reference to being in the midst of lions and ravenous beasts — symbolic language depicting cruel, treacherous and strong enemies. God's faithfulness is valid in the presence of all enemies. No enemy and no situation can keep His faithfulness away from His people. Hence, the person who trusts God and His faithfulness will "dwell in the shelter of the Most High" and "rest in the shadow of the Almighty", whose faithfulness will be a shield and rampart for the soul (Psalm 91:1, 4).

When God delivered His people from dangerous situations and enemies, it was an exhilarating moment that again reminded God's people of His faithfulness. They would sing that "the faithfulness of the Lord endures forever" (Psalm 117:2). God does not run out of faithfulness or get tired of it. His faithfulness is never diminished or diluted. It can be always trusted on.

But what happens when things become difficult for us? Has God's faithfulness waned in such circumstances? No. We must understand that God's faithfulness to us is built upon His faithfulness to His own purposes and Word. We know that His faithfulness is also related to our own ultimate good. It may not seem like that when we are going through tough times. But Scripture assures us that God's faithfulness can also result in our affliction. The psalmist sang, "in faithfulness you have afflicted me" but was comforted by the knowledge that God's unfailing love would comfort him and that God's promises are based on God's faithfulness, which works for our eternal good (Psalm 119:76) and will ultimately never fail.

If we suffer, God's love is embedded in it and His faithfulness will sustain us. God disciplines His children for their own good (Hebrews 12:7, 10). He wants us to share in His holiness and will bring us through thick and thin, but in all of it we will not be cut off from His faithfulness, for He is working all things for our own good (Romans 8:28).

God never ceases to be loving and faithful (Psalm 25:10). "He is faithful in all he does" (Psalm 33:4), and "remains faithful forever" (Psalm 146:6). This very quality of divine faithfulness was found in Jesus.

The Faithfulness of Jesus

We read in Hebrews that Jesus was faithful as God's Son (Hebrews 3:6). The Gospel accounts are rich descriptions of His unfading and wonderful faithfulness to His Father who sent Him. In all of this, Jesus reflected the faithfulness of God which was an essential part of God's character.

Jesus constantly remembered His identity and mission. Again and again, Jesus kept emphasising the truth that He was sent by the Father (John 3:17; 4:34; 5:30, 36, 38; 6:29, 38, 44; 7:16, 29; 8:16, 18, 26, 29; 8:42…). He was not operating on His own, but always saw Himself in connection with His Father, and working for and with His Father. That is the basic attitude of faithfulness. Faithfulness is rooted in a vibrant and enduring relationship. It speaks of loyalty in all situations. In an age where the only person people are faithful to is themselves, we need to observe and learn faithfulness from Jesus. We live in an age where employees are no longer as loyal to their companies as previous generations were. There are many working more for themselves than for their companies or institutions. In this self-serving commercial culture, personal benefits, security and wellbeing over-ride all other concerns.

This may be true in other relationships too. It is increasingly being seen in families, churches, neighbourhoods and nations. Loyalty only to self or more to self than to others, results in mobility — whether it has to do with transient jobs, family relationships, or citizenships. It is in this context that the faithfulness of Jesus to His Father remains a huge challenge for modern Christians.

Jesus was faithful in what He was and did. He only did what his Father told Him to say and do. "I only do what I see my Father doing" (John 5:19). "I...speak just what the Father has taught me" (John 8:28; cf. 15:15; 17:8). "I love the Father...and I do exactly what the Father has commanded me" (John 14:31). In all these statements Jesus was simply describing His perfect loyalty and faithfulness to His Father. There was not a word from the mouth of Jesus or a thought in His mind that strayed from His relationship with His Father. He was totally committed to His Father, and nothing could take away that commitment.

Jesus did only what pleased the Father. Jesus demonstrated that He was not living for His own pleasure but for the Father's pleasure. "I always do what pleases Him" (John 8:29), "I seek not to please myself but him who sent me" (John 5:30). In His unrelenting and utter obedience to His Father there was not even an iota of self-gratification. He did not take a holiday for self-indulgence. "I have come from heaven not to do my will but to do the will of him who sent me" (John 6:38; cf. Luke 22:42).

The one over-riding passion of Jesus was to glorify His Father. Jesus had a passionate desire to glorify the Father. He did not live and serve to glorify Himself. Self-glorification was not in His vocabulary, even as the Son of God. He said, "I am not seeking glory for myself" (John 8:50), "If I glorify myself my glory means nothing" (John 8:58). Jesus sought to honour and glorify His Father and was prepared to do anything to achieve this purpose. "I honor my Father" (John 8:49); "And I will do whatever you ask in my name, so that the Son may bring glory to the Father" (John 14:13).

Jesus sacrificed His life to be faithful to His Father. He knew that to bring glory to His Father He had to obey His Father even if it meant going to the cross. At the Garden of Gethsemane, He submitted Himself to what was going to be the unimaginably painful experience (and we are not simply talking about physical suffering here) of the cross where the despicable sins of the whole world were to be carried. He "became obedient to death — even death on a cross!" (Philippians 2:8).

Jesus was faithful even in the worst of sufferings. Never once did He falter in His faithfulness. He held resolutely to the steady path of faithfulness, and withstood every pain, no matter what, in order to be faithful to His Father. He was faithful to the end and completed His work for His Father on the cross: "I have brought you glory on earth by completing the work you gave me to do." (John 17:4). He faithfully reported to His Father from the cross, "It is finished" (John 19:30). He was faithful every step of the way, and to the end.

Satan, who was not God but one of the chief angels created by God, became proud, and in his pride and selfish ambition, worshipped himself and became horribly and hideously unfaithful to God. But the Son of God, who is God Himself, took the form of a servant and became obedient and faithful right to the end. What a striking contrast! Lest we are too quick to condemn Satan, we must realise that we are no better than Satan. At least he was at one time a highly respectable and splendid angel. We are merely human beings, creatures who are guilty of the same self-pride and self-worship, of the same rebelliousness and treachery against God our Creator.

Jesus stands out in His faithfulness, especially because of who He is — the eternal Son of God. The prophet Isaiah saw a glorious sight of Jesus long before Jesus stepped onto the earth. Isaiah saw a royal Branch who had faithfulness as a sash around His waist (Isaiah 11:5). Jesus fulfilled that prophecy by living faithfully during His time on earth. One of His disciples, John, in his final years, noted that Jesus was the "faithful witness" (Revelation 1:5). The faithfulness of Jesus would become legendary on earth and in heaven, and for all time. In the apocalyptic vision of the final days, Jesus is called

"Faithful and True" (Revelation 19:11). Those who seek to follow Him in this life must, therefore, reflect His faithfulness.

Living Faithfully

God was often disappointed by the faithlessness of His people. They had the benefit of God's revelation. They had God's Law and Temple. They had priests and prophets. They had God's Word. But they were faithless and were unfaithful to God (Jeremiah 3:12-14). God often depicted their unfaithfulness in terms of a marital relationship (depicting God's relationship to Israel; God being the husband and Israel the wife). Israel was a deplorably unfaithful spouse.

God repeatedly urged His faithless people to return to Him. Can we be faithful to Him? Scripture tells us that we live in a time when people are increasingly faithless (Romans 1:31). Ideas of faithfulness and loyalty are considered to be old-fashioned and outdated in an era where increasingly people are loyal only to themselves. As rapidly changing social values are seeping into every facet of life, and the church has not been spared, old ideas of faithfulness to God are being eroded.

How then can we strengthen our faithfulness and loyalty to God? We return to the same principles of surrendering to the rule of Christ in our hearts and the power of the indwelling Holy Spirit that will enable us to let Christ live in us. This will result in us bearing spiritual fruit and showing forth the character of Jesus.

> "[We] had a great deal to say about our embodiment of God's loyalty to the world in a personal and communal lifestyle of faithfulness in action. But such a lifestyle does not, and indeed cannot, emerge in and of itself. The biblical witness is very clear that loyalty can exist, however frail it is, only as a response to the communal and personal experience of God's faithfulness to us. It is God's loyalty that motivates our loyalty, that strengthens our loyalty when it falters, that corrects our loyalty when it is misplaced."[3]

We need to also work out our salvation by practising spiritual disciplines and taking steps to ensure we remain faithful to Christ.

Take Care of Your Relationship with Christ

Faithfulness has to do with loving relationships. Our faithfulness is essentially to our Lord Jesus Christ and to the triune God. If we neglect our relationship to Christ, how can we remain faithful to Him? In being called to be "faithful ones" (Psalm 97:10; 37:28), we are to remain faithful to God at all times, and God has promised to be faithful to His faithful ones, guarding them at all times. Often we overestimate our faithfulness to God, until we are tested and realise how fragile our loyalty to God is. Peter, with false confidence, promised Jesus his loyalty. Even if all others were to run away, he promised Jesus that he would stand by Him. He was even prepared to lay down his life for Jesus. But Scripture tells us that he failed miserably and ended up denying Jesus three times within a short time (Luke 22:31-34, 54-62).

Jesus restored Peter by bringing his attention to the heart of faithfulness (John 21). He asked Peter about his love for Jesus and told him to serve Him right to the end (and indicated that the end would not be pleasant). If there is no love for God, there can be no relationship with Him. Our faithfulness and loyalty to God would be as strong as our love for Him. Later, after being filled with the Holy Spirit, Peter showed wonderful faithfulness to his Lord, choosing to obey his Lord more than the powerful men of this world (Acts 4:1-22).

The old word "gumption" is usefully recovered for our reflections. It refers to a hardiness and heartiness that comes from a determination to be loyal to one's principles and commitments. It takes on risks and sticks, no matter what happens. This stickability and adhesiveness reveals firm commitment that displays courage when it is needed. Gumption will hang on even if it results in pain and death. The disciples of Jesus had gumption after they were filled with the Holy Spirit. Charles Swindoll has shown that gumption is rooted in a firm commitment, is lived out in daily discipline, watches out for subtle temptations along the way, requires accountability and finishes well.[4] This is a most helpful description of what faithfulness entails.

Faithfulness will grow in our lives if we remember our identity (not who we are, but *whose we are*). In all the moments of this life, we are to remember whose we are and then live accordingly. We are to be faithful to our Lord and the identity He has given us. We are to live faithfully as God's children, "so that you may become blameless and pure, children of God without fault in a crooked and depraved generation, in which you shine like stars in the universe as you hold out the word of life" (Philippians 2:15).

Read the Word to Obey God

Faithfulness to God is marked by obedience to Him. How can we be faithful to Him if we do not obey Him? *And how can we obey Him if we are ignorant of His Word*, through which the Spirit normally speaks to us? The psalmist declared, "I have hidden your word in my heart that I might not sin against you" (Psalm 119:11). Jesus showed how true this was when He handled the powerful and shrewdly arranged temptations of the devil by resorting to the Word of God. In each of the three temptations, Jesus resorted to Scripture. He was faithful to God because He knew and obeyed the Word. Knowledge of the Word not only helps us not to sin but also to do good and please God.

Know and Keep Your Vocation

God has called each of us to serve Him faithfully. For each, there is a specific task and specific gifts. We have to be careful of not trying to do everything, and ending up not doing the particular something that God wants us to do. Jesus Himself did not attempt to do everything possible. He was mindful of focusing on the specific work that was entrusted to Him.

A major problem with Christians is that in spite of all that they sing about and hear in church, they have embraced worldly ideas of success. Thus, many Christians have joined others in pursuing possessions, titles and achievements in their desire to be successful. True success, however, does not consist of what we have gathered by way of worldly wealth and honour. It really has to do with our being faithful to God. Mother Teresa was once asked, "How do you measure the success of your work?" She thought about the question and then, giving her interviewer a puzzled look, said, "I don't remember that the Lord ever spoke of success. He spoke only of faithfulness in love. This is the only success that really counts."[5] How much we need to hear this, for there are many Christians who, in looking for worldly success, have become unfaithful to God.

Eugene Peterson has written about the danger of busyness in life and ministry — because busyness is a sign of unfaithfulness. For him the word "busy" is "the symptom not of commitment but of betrayal...not devotion but defection."[6] We can be busy because of our personal agenda or the agenda of others. Such agendas can take us away from God's agenda for us. We can overcome this by making a habit to say "yes" firstly and primarily to God. If we are requested to do something by others, we must make it a habit to ask the Lord first. Our "yes" should be directed to God rather than the people who are making a request — because God is our ultimate Master.

When a man of God was sent by God to Bethel to prophesy against Jeroboam who rebelled against the kingdom of David, he accomplished what he was sent to do (1 Kings 14:1-32). Then Jeroboam invited the man for a meal and promised a gift, but the man of God declined because God had given him specific instructions not to stop for any meals. But an old prophet stopped him on the way and invited him for a meal, deceptively reassuring him that God had told him to invite the man for a meal. The man of God let down his guard and had a meal with the old prophet — thus becoming unfaithful to the instructions God had given him. He should have said "no" even if it was an apparently godly prophet who invited him. If he had asked God before accepting the invitation, he could have escaped from the lion that killed him. He could have told the prophet who claimed to speak for God that God had not personally told him to stop for a meal. Therefore, he should simply go his way.

Saying "no" to anything that is not of God, no matter how religious or pious it looks like, is not a sign of laziness. Laziness or indifference is when God has given us spiritual gifts and we do not use them at all. The man who buried his talent which his master gave him had no valid excuse when it was time to give an account (Matthew 25:14-30). Similarly, not using the spiritual gifts that the Holy Spirit gives variously to everyone in the Body of Christ (1 Corinthians 12) is a sign of gross disregard of what God has given and a failure or refusal to understand the call to Christian discipleship. It is unfaithfulness to God and His people. It is failure to appreciate the truth that "those who have been given a trust must prove faithful" (1 Corinthians 4:2). In this case, our previous point has to be noted in its reverse implications. If a potential ministry opportunity knocks at our door, and our personal inclination is to say "no," it is important to pray and determine what God would really have us do.

Faithfulness to God consists of using the spiritual gifts He has given in a way He has determined. It is neither uncaring laziness (that ignores spiritual obligations and is imprisoned in personal agendas) nor unthinking activism (that attempts to do everything according to personal desire or social expectations). Jesus shows us the way when He referred to "the very work that the Father has given me to finish, and which I am doing" (John 5:36).

We must serve God faithfully with all our heart (1 Samuel 12:24) if we are to hear God's words on the Day of Judgment, "Well done, good and faithful servant!" (Matthew 25:21). This involves faithfulness with regard to all that had been entrusted to us by the Lord, even in the little things. If we prove that we can be trusted for the small things, God may entrust bigger things to us (Luke 16:10-12).

These words of Evelyn Underhill, who sees faithfulness as "consecration in overalls," inspire us to be faithful even in the little things, in the daily routines of our lives:

> "The fruits of the Spirit get less and less showy as we go on. Faithfulness means continuing quietly with the job we have been given, in the situation where we have been placed; not yielding to the restless desire for change. It means tending the lamp quietly for God without wondering how much longer it has got to go on. Steady, unsensational driving, taking good

> care of the car. A lot of the road to heaven has to be taken at thirty miles per hour. It means keeping everything in your charge in good order for love's sake, rubbing up the silver, polishing the glass even though you know the Master will not be looking round the pantry next weekend. If your life is really part of the apparatus of the Spirit, that is the sort of life it must be. You have got to be the sort of cat who can be left alone with the canary; the sort of dog who follows, hungry and thirsty but tail up to the end of the day.
>
> Faithfulness and Goodness—they are doggy qualities. Fancy that as a Fruit of the Spirit! But then the Spirit is Love, and doggy love is a very good sort of love, humble and selfless and enduring...In the interior life of prayer, faithfulness points steadily to God and His purposes, away from self and its preoccupations."[7]

There is a doggedness about faithfulness and a godliness about it that is firmly rooted in God's will and obedience to God.

Be Faithful in Prayer

Prayer is a relationship with God and its constant practice helps to deepen that relationship. Prayer is not just bringing a shopping list of petitions to God so that we can live comfortable, trouble-free and successful lives. No, prayer is much deeper than that for the pulse of prayer is a desire for God's presence. To neglect prayer is to neglect our relationship with God — an evidence that we have forgotten our first love. A prayerless life or a life with scattered superficial prayers is a path to unfaithfulness. Hence Paul urges his readers to be "faithful in prayer" (Romans 12:12). Like Daniel, we must not allow social or any other decrees to change our habits of faithful praying (Daniel 6:10). Unfortunately, one of the first things in our lives that is sacrificed in the midst of busyness or success is prayer.

Faithfulness to God and all that is in the heart of God, to the work He has given us and to His people, is a fruit of the Holy Spirit. It will emerge in our life as we live in Christ and are filled with the Holy Spirit. It can be bruising and may hurt, for often there is a price to pay for such faithfulness. It will involve crucifying our sinful nature with all its desires and crucifying ourselves from the world (Galatians 5:24; 6:14). When the temptations are great and the trials fiery, we would hear God saying, "Be faithful, even to the point of death, and I will give you the crown of life" (Revelation 2:10). Countless martyrs have heard this and proven it true. Paul, who was one of them, wrote towards the end of his faithful life, "I have fought the good fight. I have finished the race. I have kept the faith" (2 Timothy 4:7). Fought, finished, kept. Such a life of faithfulness is a truly beautiful life and brings glory to the faithful God whose faithfulness endures forever.

Questions for Reflection

1. What lessons can we learn from God on faithfulness? How does God show His covenantal faithfulness? In what way is God's faithfulness directed at those who are inferior or weak and marginalised? What is the implication of this for our own lives?

2. How did Jesus show faithfulness in life and ministry? How did Jesus show that He was "faithful and true" (Revelation 19:11)? What can we learn from Jesus?

3. How is faith in God and faithfulness to Him connected? Why is it not possible to have one without the other? How can you grow in the way you trust and obey God?

4. What spiritual habits can build our faithfulness — to God and others? What social factors hinder such faithfulness and how can you deepen your reliance on the Spirit to be more faithful?

11

GENTLENESS: THE BEAUTY OF LOVE

The eighth aspect of the fruit of the Holy Spirit is gentleness. The original Greek word is *prautēs*, which has been variously translated in English Bibles as gentleness and meekness, both of which carry similar connotations.

One of the difficulties we face is that the English words "gentleness" and "meekness" have become culturally diluted over time and now popularly connote weakness. Stephen Winward explains such popular distortions when he writes about these commonly held ideas: "Meekness is weakness. The meek man, so we imagine, is timid and feeble, spineless and incapable. He is lacking in energy and virality, in drive and aggression. He is the kind of person who wouldn't say boo to a goose — a doormat, exploited by all, who submits tamely to injury. No one could possibly desire to be such a milk-and-watery person, such an ineffectual creature."[1]

Hollywood depictions of hapless men with clerical collars, standing meekly in the background as life goes on, further feed into this distorted notions of biblical meekness. This cannot be further from the truth. Winward is right in pointing out that biblical meekness and gentleness is "strength under control." He explains, "This combination of strength and restraint, of power possessed but under control, and that out of regard for the welfare of others, is true gentleness."[2]

Paul Willis agrees with this understanding when he defines meekness by tracing the etymological roots of the English word "gentleman."

> "Meekness has a twofold expression. Toward God, it issues in complete trust and submission to God. Meekness is to be mastered by the will of God. It results in gentleness, consideration, courtesy. It is strength under control. Meekness is the character of the one who has the power to retaliate, yet remains kind. It is from such a spirit that the expression gentle-man or gentleman arises.
>
> Meekness is an attitude toward God which manifests itself in gentleness towards others. It is an attitude of submission and yieldedness to God which results in the harnessing of our strength in godly ways toward our fellow man. It is a love that seeks first not its own, but the things of God and others. The meek accept God's will and dealings without sulking, rebellion, or resistance."[3]

Meekness is therefore not weakness or the absence of power and authority. Jesus illustrated this when He washed His disciples' feet before going on to the cross (John 13:1-17). The text notes that "Jesus knew that the Father had put all things under his power" (John 13:3). Jesus was in total control and absolutely in charge. The ESV Bible puts it this way: "Jesus, knowing that the Father had given all things into his hands..." All power and authority were in the hands of Jesus. And yet, those very hands gently washed the dirt off the feet of the puzzled and uncomfortable disciples. That, indeed, is a wonderful picture, not only of humility but also of gentleness. Instead of crushing the feet of unreliable men (and even those of a treacherous man), the powerful hands of the God-Man handled those sinful feet with divine gentleness.

Jesus said that He has set an example for us to follow (John 13:15), and in this chapter we must ask how we can understand this more deeply (in terms of gentleness) and do this in practice. We must remember and take note that the gentleness of Jesus reflects the gentleness of God.

yoke is not an instrument of torture; it is an instrument of mercy. It is not a malicious contrivance for making work hard; it is a gentle device to make hard labor light. It is not meant to give pain, but to save pain."[4] This is reminiscent of what is said of the Messiah — that "a bruised reed he will not break and a smoldering wick he will not snuff out" (Isaiah 42:3), which was fulfilled in Jesus as noted by Matthew (Matthew 12:20). The Jews had great difficulties in understanding and appreciating this picture of a gentle Messiah, for they expected a Messiah on a royal war horse, not on a humble donkey — even though Scripture had prophesied about this:

> "Rejoice greatly, O daughter of Zion! Shout, Daughter of Jerusalem! See your king comes to you, righteous and having salvation, gentle and riding on a donkey, on a colt, the foal of a donkey" (Zechariah 9:9).

The gentle Messiah would ride into Jerusalem on a donkey, not in severe fiery judgment, and die on the cross in self-surrendering love. The gentleness was such a characteristic aspect of the way Jesus lived and ministered that Paul when writing to the fractious and rather chaotic church in Corinth appealed by the "meekness and gentleness of Christ" (2 Corinthians 10:1).

The Gentle Teacher

Jesus taught in His Sermon on the Mount, "Blessed are the meek [*prautēs*] for they will inherit the earth" (Matthew 5:5), reiterating what the Old Testament had already declared (Psalm 37:11). Jesus dealt with His disciples gently on the many occasions when they responded to His teachings with a frustrating lack of understanding and faith. There were times when Jesus told parables, and like the crowds, the disciples failed to understand. They had to have private tuition with Jesus who had to patiently and gently explain the meaning of the parable to them (Matthew 13:1-23). Any student who has encountered a harsh and impatient teacher would appreciate how Jesus dealt gently with His exasperatingly slow disciples.

The Gentle Healer and Minister

Jesus dealt gently with the weak and infirm. The powerful hands of Jesus touched lepers, children, the blind and the lame with great compassion. A synagogue ruler by the name of Jairus had a 12-year old daughter (his only daughter) who was dying. He approached and begged Jesus to do something. By the time they reached the man's house, the girl had tragically died. Jesus went to her and "took her by the hand" (Luke 8:53). With all three Synoptic Gospels mentioning this, it must have had been a striking sight — perhaps it was the way Jesus held the dead girl's hand gently and compassionately.

Jesus was gentle with the children. He welcomed them and "took the children in his arms, put his hands on them and blessed them (Mark 10:16) — we can easily imagine how gently He must have done this. On another occasion, when He noted that His disciples had been arguing about who among them was the greatest, Jesus took a little child in His arms and taught them an important lesson (Mark 9:33-37). Greatness is measured differently in the Kingdom of God. Welcoming a little child was like welcoming Jesus. Even a little child is important in the Kingdom and must be treated well. As Jesus spoke, He must have held the child gently and smiled at him or her. It is good to meditate on such poignant biblical scenes.

What about the Cleansing of the Temple by Jesus?

This event is recorded by all the Synoptic Gospels (Matthew 21:12-16, Mark 11:15-18; Luke 19:45-47). It took place after the triumphant entry of Jesus into Jerusalem, during the last week of His life on earth. John places a similar incident at the beginning of the ministry of Jesus (John 2:13-16) after His first miracle. Did Jesus lose His cool and temper when He cleared the temple of all the ungodly business that was going on in the temple grounds? Those in power were making money exchanging ordinary currency for temple money at exorbitant rates, using the image of Caesar on the normal coins (which they said would desecrate the temple) as an excuse for their greedy enterprise. Animals for sacrifice were to be purchased only with temple currency. It was such a roaring business that the Court of the Gentiles was filled with the tables of money changers and benches and tables for selling sacrificial animals.

The noise and the greed must have been despicable to Jesus. The Court of the Gentiles, which should have reminded and demonstrated to the Jews that they worshipped the God whose house shall be a house of prayer for all nations (Isaiah 56:7) had become distorted and defiled by the narrow greedy desires of those who were making the temple a lucrative business instead of being a house for mission and prayer.

It is easy to understand why Jesus reacted with righteous anger. But did He lose His temper? There are a couple of points we must note.

Firstly, Jesus never raged and ranted. He was always gentle. We must keep in mind what divine gentleness is — strength under control. Jesus never lost control of Himself.

Secondly, we must constantly correct wrong notions of biblical gentleness created by popular culture.

In the face of gross abuse of a religious institution like the temple or gross disregard for the character and mission of God, we cannot expect Jesus to be mild and smiling and do politically correct things. He spoke out and acted out of concern for the truth of God. Gentleness does not mean that we need to abandon truth for silly and unfaithful compromises. It does not mean that we cannot tell the truth or stand for justice. It means that we should always reflect the gentleness of God even when we are upset.

Perhaps we would understand this when we consider the advice given to parents by experts. When you have to discipline your child, never lose your temper. Do not dump your anger on your children. But this does not mean that you should not correct your child and discipline him. Acting with rage leads to child abuse. Not acting at all is to abandon being a good and responsible parent and to confuse being permissively mild with being gentle.

The problem may be the little detail that John provides. Jesus made a "whip out of cords" and used it when he cleared the temple grounds. People usually imagine Him using it to beat the greedy businessmen. But the text says that He used it to drive the sheep and cattle away (John 2:15). He did not beat the poor animals but he drove them away. Was He abusive? No. Did He make His point? Yes. Was He gentle? Yes, if gentleness is strength held in restraint, for He could have done far more deadly things than simply overturning tables and chasing animals out of the temple area.

We close this section with a further point about the gentleness of Jesus. His gentleness held together His power and His considerate control of it — demonstrated again and again, whether He was dealing with innocent children, the weak and sick, or smart business people in religious premises. Decades after His resurrection, Jesus met with His disciple John. John saw Jesus in all His awesome holiness. It was such an awesome sight that John "fell at his feet as though dead" (Revelation 1:17). Who can blame him? But what the awesome Jesus did at that point is most telling. John described it in these words: "Then he placed his hand on me and said: 'Do not be afraid'" (Revelation 1:17).

John saw Jesus holding seven stars in His right hand; the stars were angels connected with the churches (Revelation 1:16, 20). However we interpret this, we can all say that the right hand of Jesus is depicted with power and authority, in line with His awesome and frightening presence. It is this same right hand that touches the frightened John. Imagine the scene, and note the gentleness of Jesus — strength and power under considerate control.

Living Gentle Lives

As followers of Jesus and the children of God, filled with the Holy Spirit, we are to display the same gentleness of Jesus that we find in Him. How are we to do this? We must always return to the basic principle of the surrendered life lived in Christ and filled with the Holy Spirit. We must remember, as Jerry Bridges reminds us, that "It takes strength, God's strength to be truly gentle."[5] This will bring a gentleness that has a lot to do with the ability to listen — to God and others. Adrian van Kaam's prayer-poem reflects this well:

"Lord, let me find back
The lost treasure of time:
Time for gentle listening to a friend...
Let me not cram every moment
With useful or exciting things
To do or say.
Let my life be a gentle preparation
For the pure and precious moments
Of listening to you
So that I may not drown
In the rushing waters
Of practical pursuits."[6]

Such a life will bring forth the character of Christ. For the Christian, this includes showing the gentleness of Christ in all his or her dealings. We are urged by Paul to live Spirit-filled, mature and gentle lives. "I urge you to live a life worthy of the calling you have received. Be completely humble and gentle; be patient, bearing with one another in love" (Ephesians 4:1-2). What would a completely gentle person be like? He would be like Jesus, and his gentleness would be the gentleness of divine love.

Gentleness has a lot to do with humility, as we can observe in the life of Jesus and in the teachings of Paul. Humility puts the self in the background and marginalises it so that we can pay attention to others and treat them as creations of God. Such humility is possible only with the grace of God. As Iris Murdoch reminds us, it is not common, even among Christians:

> "Humility is a rare virtue and an unfashionable one and one which is often hard to discern. Only rarely does one meet somebody in whom it positively shines, in whom one apprehends with amazement the absence of the anxious avaricious tentacles of the self...The humble man, because he sees himself as nothing, can see other things as they are."[7]

Humility in the presence of God and others will be the fertile ground on which gentleness can grow by the grace of God and as we cooperate with that grace. Such Christian gentleness can and ought to be shown in the various areas of our lives.

Gentleness at Home

Peter exhorted his readers to exercise Christian character at home (1 Peter 3:1-7). Wives were to be submissive to their husbands while husbands were to be considerate in the way they relate with their wives. Wives were reminded that if they had unbelieving husbands, they had a better chance of winning over their husbands to the faith through their conduct (if the husband refuses to accept his Christian wife's words). If the eloquence of their language would not win their husbands, then the example of their lives would.

This meant that the wives should focus on building their character and not waste time enhancing their appearance. They should be more concerned about their character than their cosmetics, their virtues than their wardrobes, with their inward attitudes than their outward adornment. In this regard, Peter contrasts the superficial skin-deep and clothes-deep attractiveness to the "unfading beauty of a gentle and quiet spirit, which is of great worth in God's sight" (1 Peter 3:4). True beauty has to do with Christlike character. In particular, gentleness shines with godly beauty. This has to be shown in daily interactions at home.

What is true for women is also true for men. They are also to show gentleness at home. Husbands are exhorted to be considerate to their wives and to "treat them with respect as the weaker partner" (1 Peter 3:7). The idea of the "weaker partner" has to do with physical strength and not psychological or spiritual concepts. Because men are physically bigger and stronger, they are to exercise gentleness in the way they treat their wives. They are to be considerate. We recall that gentleness is strength held in considerate control. Power (whether physical or social) is to be used with gentleness. Otherwise it will give rise to bullying, abuse, even violence.

Family relationships are supposed to be marked by tenderness. Unfortunately the closest relationships in life can also be the most hurtful and abusive. In a time when harshness and abuse (spurred on by rampant individualism and self-indulgent consumerism) is on the rise, it is so important that the beauty of gentleness be practised at home. Parents are never to vent their anger on their children when they discipline them. They should never discipline their child when they are not in control of their emotions. One can never be gentle if one's strength is not under one's control.

Parents must not join the harshness of the world by making unreasonable demands on their children, pushing them beyond breaking point. They must have time to have real conversations and practise gentleness in their speech. Whoever has power in the family over the others must use the power to build and minister rather than to hurt and destroy. Power held in considerate control is gentleness. The practice of gentleness is often replicated. Gentleness will beget gentleness, while harshness will similarly be reproduced.

Gentleness in Church

As children of God we are also to live with gentleness in the church. Unfortunately some of the worst fights and examples of harshness can be found in the church, especially when the church is rife with dysfunctional relationships and sin. Self-interests, pride, envy, anger, the fight for power, majoring on the minor — these and other reasons often lie behind such sad behaviour in church.

One of the big difficulties in church is the inability to relate with sinners and knowing how to deal with them. If everyone pretends that everyone is living alright, then sinners who have been exposed have no place in such a pretentious place. The gut instinct is to treat the sinner harshly and cruelly. Such was the case when some teachers of the law and Pharisees brought a woman caught in adultery to Jesus. They not only shamed the woman publicly, but also asked what Jesus thought of stoning her according to the Law. Jesus quietly wrote on the ground with His finger and challenged them, "If any one of you is without sin, let him be the first to throw a stone at her" (John 8:7).

Perhaps they stood there with stones in their hands, ready to put an end to the despicable sinner. But Jesus had exposed their hypocrisy and sinfulness. The older ones left first, perhaps because the longer you live, the more sins you have committed (and the more you can remember). Soon, none of them was left. It was then that Jesus asked the women whether anyone had condemned her. When she replied, "No one sir," He told her, "Then neither do I condemn you...Go now and leave your life of sin" (John 8:10-11). Jesus dealt with the sinner firmly but gently.

Paul urges us to follow and emulate Jesus. To the Galatians he wrote, "Brothers, if someone is caught in a sin, you who are spiritual should restore him *gently*" (Galatians 6:1, emphasis added). The purpose is to restore the fallen brother with discipline, not to destroy him with punishment. This was a point unappreciated by the Corinthian Christians who treated a sinful believer in church in extreme ways, firstly overlooking and tolerating his sin in an irresponsible and ungodly way, and then later expelling him, ignoring him and leaving him unrestored (1 Corinthians 5; 2 Corinthians 2:5-11).

Here Paul urges us to treat those who have fallen into sin with gentleness. What does this mean? It means that we should use the power and authority given to us with great care, always seeking the good of the other person, and treating him with gentleness.

In the case of pastors having to deal with difficult members, Paul's principle applies. How does one deal with those who oppose your authority? Paul's instruction to Timothy is clear enough: "And the Lord's servant must not be quarrelsome but must be kind to everyone, able to teach, not resentful. Opponents must be gently instructed, in the hope that God will grant them repentance leading them to a knowledge of the truth, and that they will come to their senses and escape from the trap of the devil, who has taken them captive to do his will" (2 Timothy 2:24-26). Those who are quarrelsome and (wrongly and unreasonably) oppose the pastor are to be "gently instructed." Just think of what that entails. Instruction can be harsh but it can also be gentle; it is obvious which type of instruction has a greater chance of winning over the erring brother.

Moses in the Old Testament was given authority by God to lead the people of Israel out of Egypt and through the desert into the promised land. However his authority and leadership were questioned on several occasions. Each time the people rose and rebelled against him, Moses responded in a godly way by "falling facedown" (Numbers 14:5; 16:4), meaning that He responded with humble prayer to God (as he did in Exodus 15:25 when he "cried out" to the Lord as the thirsty people grumbled against Moses). Even his own brother and sister opposed Moses at one point and criticised him. Apparently he said nothing and God had to intervene on behalf of him. Of Moses, the text says this: "Now the man Moses was very meek, more than all people who were on the face of the earth" (Numbers 12:3, ESV). We can learn much from the way Moses used his authority and practised meekness and gentleness.

Gentleness in the World

As it is, we live in a harsh and unforgiving world. Try driving on the congested highway on a busy weekday morning. Or go to the workplace where demands come through all your technological marvels (mobiles, emails), expecting instant attention. Or think of the way people treat people in the many spheres of life: at official counters, in neighbourhood precincts, in war-zones. It is easy to imbibe the patterns of behaviour and start believing that one has to be harsh to survive in a harsh world.

This cannot be further from the truth, for the words of Jesus keep challenging us. It is the meek who will inherit the earth (Matthew 5:5). We are to live out of this gentleness that is a characteristic of Jesus. It means that those of us who have power and authority over others must use them with respect and consideration for others. We must not abuse these, for we will then end up abusing others. This happens all the time, when employers cheat their employees, or abuse their domestic maids, or when corrupt officials send poor people around on an uncaring and unreasonable wild-goose chase when they come seeking for help.

Not so for the Christian. In all situations, we are to exercise gentleness. Even when others who are different from us, especially those of other faiths or no faith, approach us to discuss our faith, we are to treat them with gentleness and respect. Peter's ancient advice is most relevant for us today. "But in your hearts revere Christ as Lord. Always be prepared to give an answer to everyone who asks you to give the reason for the hope that you have. But do this with gentleness and respect" (1 Peter 3:15, NIV). Gentleness is to be exercised even (and especially) if others do not share our views.

When we live with such gentleness, it will have good consequences. If we cannot win over others with our winsome words, we may win them over with our winsome lives. The beauty of gentleness has a powerful testimony on its own. It also makes the world a more liveable place, a kinder and gentler place for all.

"Praise you, Lord,
For your splendid promise
To send the Spirit
Light of light,
The gracious One
Whose radiation
Pierces like a lazer beam
The wall we build
Around our hearts.
Lovely Spirit of the Lord
Dim the turmoil
Of frenzied words.
Clean away the arrogance
That pollutes the atmosphere
Of gentleness and love.
Temper our self-assertion,
Soften our unbending stand,
Save us from deceptive dealings,

From policies of lust and pride.
Enlighten us, confused and caught
In argument and angry thought."[8]

We will do well if we can pray the above prayer for gentleness in our lives (as opposed to aggression) — slowly, repeatedly, and deeply. Trusting God's grace to enable us to become gentle must be accompanied by the practice of spiritual disciplines that will help us in the process. Using the image of life as a tapestry, Judith Lechman describes how gentleness is woven into the whole tapestry of life:

> "Imagine our tapestry one last time, whole, complete and glowing with that fruit of the Spirit called gentleness. What would we see in this our final glance at the creation of the divine? We would see God's design and our craftsmanship, his will and our obedience, his call and our answer, his command and our fulfilment of it. We would see gentleness as we initially sought it, then struggled for it, and lastly, worked to live it in every aspect of our life. And we would know the wholeness that comes with having done our best to be faithful to the gentle Artist who creates the tapestry that is life."[9]

The story of how gentleness is produced in our lives as we cooperate and struggle with God's grace is the story of how God sanctifies, transforms and perfects us. As far as gentleness is concerned, we will become godly and gentle people as we submit ourselves to God's grace. Instead of abusive relationships where we abuse others (and even the environment), we will reflect the gentleness of God whose gentle power touches us not to destroy but to redeem and bless.

Questions for Reflection

1. Discuss what Christian gentleness is and is not. What popular misconceptions exist concerning gentleness? How is gentleness connected with power?

2. In what ways is God gentle? Discuss the gentleness of Jesus and how it was shown. How would you explain the cleansing of the temple by Jesus in relation to the quality of gentleness (Matthew 21:12-16)? What can we learn from Jesus?

3. What would a completely gentle person be like (Ephesians 4:1-2)? Why is it necessary to surrender to Christ and rely on the Spirit in the process of becoming gentle? Share how you practise this and what you have discovered from your experience.

4. Discuss the need for gentleness at home, in church, and in the world? What factors hinder the practice and development of the virtue of gentleness? How can they be overcome?

12

SELF CONTROL: WHEN LOVE SUBMITS TO GOD

The ninth and final characteristic of the fruit of the Holy Spirit is self-control. The original Greek word is *egkrateia* which means "the mastery of one's own desires and impulses."[1] Charles Swindoll defines the word as an "inner power of strength" which includes "such things as having mastery or possession of something, the controlling power of the will (under the operation of the Holy Spirit), the inner strength to resist and refrain, the strength *not* to indulge, *not* to act on impulse."[2] Scripture repeatedly emphasises the need for self-control, giving examples of when self-control is not exercised and of how the restraint of self and the discipline involved in it can bring many blessings.

Understanding Self-Control

A good example of one who lived his life without self-control was the Old Testament character of Samson. His birth was very promising — with the visit of an angel of God (perhaps a theophany, a visitation of God Himself) to his infertile parents to announce his birth (Judges 13). After his birth, we hear promising words again: "He grew and the Lord blessed him, and the Spirit of the Lord began to stir him" (Judges 23:24-25). This is reminiscent of how the birth and childhood of several people in the Bible are described, for example, Samuel (1 Samuel 2:26; 3;19), John the Baptist (Luke 1:80) and Jesus Himself (Luke 2:40).

Samson's Lack of Self-Control

Samson had many good things going for him. He had godly parents, God was there right from the beginning, he was set apart for God and was to live as a Nazirite for life (which meant that he was to live a pure life and stay away from fermented drink and touching anything unclean, such as an animal carcass, and he was not allowed to use a razor to cut his hair).

Yet trouble brewed as the story moved quickly from Samson's childhood to his adult years. He saw a Philistine woman and desired her. He told his father, "Get her for me, for she is right in my eyes" (Judges 14:3, ESV). We have here an indication to one of his basic problems — his eyes. He lived by instinct, whatever he fancied at that moment. The whole story about him is one of a man well-endowed (for he had great physical strength) but who could not even control himself. He lived by instinct and impulse, and his life was one of rage and violence. That he had problems with the uncontrolled desire of his eyes is further illustrated by accounts of his many relationships (Judges 16:1, 4). Eventually, he lost his hair due to the treachery of Delilah, and therefore lost his tremendous strength.

As a prisoner of the Philistines, Samson lost his eyes, the cause of many of his problems — his eyes were gouged out (Judges 16:21). But with slowly restored strength, he brings out his energy in one last explosion and managed to literally bring down the house and kill his Philistine tormentors. No doubt, God provided Samson's strength and used it for His larger purposes, but the text indicates that Samson was merely a *channel* for God's power but not a *vessel* for godliness. He had charisma but little character. He was a messy collection of powers, instincts, appetites, and indulgences — with very little to show by way of virtues and discipline. He was, sadly, not in control of himself.

The Difference between Stoicism and Biblical Self-Control

When we come to the New Testament, we meet Paul, a highly disciplined man. He advised his readers, "Run in such a way as to get the prize" (1 Corinthians 9:24). Paul used the illustration of athletics —when athletes prepared themselves for the Games by going through "strict training" they stood a good chance to win the race. The lack of discipline can never bring victory. Paul further wrote about how he applied this principle in his own life: "Therefore I do not run like a man running aimlessly; I do not fight like a man beating the air. No, I beat my body and make it my slave, so that after I have preached to others, I myself will not be disqualified for the prize" (1 Corinthians 9:26-27).

In living in this manner, was Paul a Stoic? Stoicism, founded by Zeno (335-263 BC) was one of the major branches of ancient Greek philosophy. While Stoicism went through historical adjustments, the popular concept was to bear life's changing circumstances bravely and remain virtuous till the end. On the surface, this may sound similar to the spirituality of Paul and Peter when they urge their readers to patiently bear with suffering and not lose their virtue. However, the ethics of the Christian faith and that of Stoicism are vastly different because they are based on vastly different worldviews. Stoicism is based on a materialistic pantheism that does not see anything beyond the material universe and beyond death. Everett Ferguson puts it well when he writes: "Self-respect, not love, was stoicism's driving force...For Stoicism...the goal of humanity is self-liberation, and this goal is attainable. It did not know the redemptive love of a merciful God."[3]

The Stoic's reference point is always the self and nothing beyond it. Paul's reference point was always God. He controlled and subjected his body to discipline (which superficially appears to be like that of the Stoic but is profoundly different) not to ultimately liberate himself but to keep himself *faithful* to God. The body that Paul subjected to control, is the "temple of the Holy Spirit" (1 Corinthians 6:19) and therefore must be worthy of being in that state. Christian self-control only makes sense in the light of our relationship with God. Hence we are to offer our bodies as "living sacrifices, holy and pleasing to God" (Romans 12:1). The body must be brought under the reign of Christ because it belongs to Him.

The mind too is to be trained like an athlete. Christian discipleship and lazy minds do not go together. Paul wrote the inspiring words, "we take captive every thought to make it obedient to Christ" (2

Corinthians 10:5). As it is for the thoughts of our minds, so it is for the emotions of our heart: "Do not let the sun go down while you are still angry, and do not give the devil a foothold" (Ephesians 4:26-27). Paul's admonishment suggests that we can and should do something about angry feelings. We must not play willing hosts to them and let them take root in our hearts, for they will do much damage.

The key conclusion we must state at this point is that self-control is a necessity for growth in Christian maturity. However we must understand that Christian self-control is not so much self-mastery as it is being mastered by Christ. Biblical self-control is not ruling ourselves but allowing ourselves to be ruled by Christ, denying sinful expressions of appetites, impulses and instincts.

Jesus and Self-Control

In what way is self-control a characteristic of God? This is not an easy question to answer in that God's self, as we would understand it, is not like our human selves which are riddled with duplicities, deception, tensions and fragmentation. We human beings have a sinful self with its sinful propensities, always urging us to sin and rebel against God. It is proud, rebellious and sinfully independent, and seeks to glorify and indulge itself. Against it we have to fight. From young we experience this fight when we have to learn how to negotiate between personal desire and social expectation, between what we feel like doing at the moment and what others expect of us. Toilet training in infancy is only the beginning of many complicated nuances in life that one must learn in order to live fairly well in society.

When we come to our relationship with God, we have to deal not only with what we desire and what others desire, but what God wants. Can we learn from the character of God in these struggles? Here we encounter a good measure of mystery. God has no problems with His self the way we do. He does not need to control Himself, for He has no uncontrollable thoughts or feelings. There is no rebellion within God, and the Persons of the Trinity are in perfect harmony with each other, each giving Himself so perfectly to the others that perfect self-giving eliminates any necessity for self-control. We could explore this further to learn some lessons, but we would do better if we go to Jesus, the God-Man.

Jesus was born as a man and identified with the human race. While the exact details of how His divine part and His human part merged together into His personality has been debated endlessly throughout the church's history, we shall simply observe that Jesus as a man, had the possibility of sinning in His thoughts, emotions and choices. Scripture testifies that He was in fact "tempted in every way just as we are — yet was without sin" (Hebrews 4:15). Specific temptations are recorded in the Gospels (Matthew 4:1-11; Luke 4:1-13). Jesus fasted for 40 days and was hungry — we can imagine how hungry. Every fibre in Him must have craved for food when Satan tempted Him to turn the desert into a giant bakery. Jesus exercised control over His hungry body, seeking to be obedient to His Father alone. He refused to be tempted "to define life in consumer terms and then devise plans and programs to accomplish them."[4]

Jesus was tempted to jump off the high point and to put up a great magic show that would impress the people. It was a moment's impulse. Why not? But Jesus restrained Himself from embracing half-baked ideas and acting on impulses (arising from Satan's seductive whispers). He refused to be pushed off the edge by impulses (even if they were superficially connected with thoughts about God) and be tempted "to embark on a circus career in miracles."[5] Centuries later, Ignatius of Loyola advised that we have to examine not only the beginning of a thought but also its middle and end, for Satan is an expert in hijacking what may begin as a noble thought.[6] There is the ever-present problem of the Christian mind which is too lazy to think and reflect and which surrenders (dangerously) to impulses and impressions rather than to the clear teaching of the Word.

Then Satan turned into a slick and convincing salesman and offered the whole world as a free gift if only Jesus would bow down and worship Him. Jesus again had total control of Himself and refused to succumb to the temptation. Eugene Peterson sees this temptation as trying "to rule from a throne-bureaucracy of abstract rules and disembodied principles imposed on men and women apart from relational trust and worshipping love."[7] Satan is a master in selling forbidden stuff. He knows all about impulsive buying — like what many people do when they are tempted to buy things they do not need and about which they will later have regrets, all because they lost self-control when tempted.

Jesus displayed total self-control because He lived not to please Himself, but only His Father (John 5:30). He lived in absolute submission to His Father for He kept saying, "not as I will but as you will" (Matthew 26:39).

When we surrender ourselves to Jesus in the same way, we will then display that same self-control.

The Self-Controlled Life

Much is said in the Bible about the need for the self-controlled life. In the Pastoral Epistles, self-control is repeatedly emphasised. For example, in his epistle to Titus, Paul insisted that elders in the church must be self-controlled (Titus 1:8). This is an important quality for leadership positions in church. This virtue will prevent several vices and destructive sinful habits that are also listed in Paul's requirements — that elders must not be quick-tempered, prone to drunkenness and violence (Titus 1:7). These are all problems that fundamentally arise as a lack of self-control.

Not only is self-control a requirement for church leadership, but it is also required of all church members: the older men — and by implication, older women (Titus 2:2), the younger women (Titus 2:5) and the younger men (Titus 2:6). That this is an inclusive requirement for all believers is emphasised in Paul's general exhortation that since God's grace has appeared to "all men" we are called "to live self-controlled, upright and godly lives in this present age" (Titus 2:11-12).

This Present Age

Self control is to be practised by the Christian in "this present age."

What sort of age do we live in? We live in a world of addictions, uncontrollable appetites, impulsive living and the self-indulgent pursuit of our own desires. Charles Swindoll adds his accurately colourful description: "The overindulgence and underachievement of our age have created a monster whose brain is lazy, vision is blurred, hands are greedy, skin is thin, middle is round, and seat is wide."[8]

In the last few centuries, one by one, authorities that have governed our lives (church, tradition, moral worldviews and the like) have been discarded as repressive and evil. We are taught to pursue our own desires and not let anything govern us. Freedom is seen as pursuing our own dreams and whims and fancies, without interference or sermonising from others. There is also the romantic notion that culture has repressed human nature, that there is something freeing and beautiful in the noble savage who lives an unrestrained life. A lot of this has to do with Western delusions arising from their rejection of older worldviews and the search for newer ones.

The result of these movements is that we have idealised the self and its instincts — as is evident in slogans popularised by advertisement mantras such as "just do it" and "obey your thirst." Increasingly we see signs of loss of self-control on a massive scale — whether it has to do with epidemic explosions of obesity, drug addictions, uncontrolled consumption, marital unfaithfulness, violent acts, road rage, uncouth and aggressive language and the like. Paul's descriptions of how people would behave in the last days is an accurate prediction of how things seem to be deteriorating in terms of human misbehaviour (Romans 1:29-31; 2 Timothy 3:2-5). We must note that Paul specifically mentions that in the last days people will be "without self-control" (2 Timothy 3:3).

The modern environment, including media, shopping, the arts, and popular culture, as a whole tends to inculcate an ethos of consumerism and voracious consumption. Greed, aggression, lust and violence are promoted endlessly in movies and the internet. Our age is represented not only by over-consumption and waste, but also increasing addictions to substances and experiences. From harmful addictions to gambling in increasingly lucrative casinos, to the everyday addiction to emails, social media, internet games and pornography — these are all symptoms of the rampant outbreak of addictive behaviours and the loss of self-control.

How then should a Christian learn to live in such an addictive and self-indulgent culture? We can think of a few important points.

Practise Temperance

There are many God-given appetites that are meant to be used in the proper circumstances and within natural and reasonable limits. Take, for instance, eating. Hunger is a natural instinct and is satisfied by eating, which can also be a pleasurable experience. However, if it is overdone, it will harm the person's health as well as social life. It would be harmful to eat all the time, to eat the wrong kind of food or to overeat.

The same principles apply when it comes to sexual needs. God has given in His Word a proper context for sexual needs to be met — within marriage — so that it does not do harm to persons unlike when it is abused. When sexual practice is dissociated from marriage it brings harm. Paul teaches that some men are gifted by God to remain single while others are gifted for marriage (1 Corinthians 7:7). He argues that in whichever case the principle is this: "I will not be mastered by anything" (1 Corinthians 6:12). The sexual drive is not meant to be abused outside of marriage because the body is the "temple of the Holy Spirit" and is not meant for "sexual immorality" (1 Corinthians 6:13). Therefore the sexual drive is meant to find expression only within the loving marital relationship. Husband and wife are encouraged to fulfil their marital responsibilities. Even if they were to restrain themselves from sexual expression for a special season of prayer they are to be mindful of their drives and live in a reasonable way as Satan can tempt them "because of your lack of self-control" (1 Corinthians 7:5).

Be Free from Addictions

In a world of addictions this is wise and practical pastoral advice. We are to avoid getting into situations or doing something that would lead us to a loss of self-control. Whether it is lust, gambling or internet gaming, we have to understand the addictive process. Psychologists have clearly shown the neurological and psychological pathways to addiction.[9] A certain behaviour gives pleasure for a while. When it wanes, the pressure to repeat the behaviour pattern increases until it is repeated. If this goes on repeatedly an addictive cycle is created and the person is trapped in it, feeling helpless and powerless. Powerful addictions often begin as innocuous little actions. Therein lies the danger.

Paul calls such sinful addiction bondage and slavery and declares that sin shall not be our master (Romans 6:14). In our baptism we have been united with Jesus and therefore have access to His resurrection power. But it also involves dying to sin. We are buried into death (Romans 6:4) — an expression that points to spiritual realities. It is strange that here the burial precedes death (which is not the normal case when people die); it in fact points to our spiritual need to *choose* to die to our sins and the desires of the flesh. This involves crucifying the old self (Romans 6:6) so that the sinful self is put to death and kept dead. When an alcoholic sees a liquor bottle, his addiction is aroused and he longs for another drink. But when he is dead, you can show him all the liquor bottles in the world, but he would not respond. To become free from sin and addiction is a similar process. It is to become dead to sin and its allurements. We do this by "starving" the sinful impulses — by learning to repeatedly say "no" to them, by denying the self and its evil desires.

Coffee drinkers with diabetes will share that when they cut down the sugar in their coffees, initially it may take some adjusting to. But if they keep a disciplined approach to it, soon they will get accustomed to drinking their coffee without sugar or with very little sugar. If one were to accidentally or ignorantly pour too much sugar in their coffee (like they were used to before cutting down their sugar) they may find the cup distasteful. Similar principles are operational when we are making efforts to develop virtues and erode vices in our lives. In practice this means taking practical and wise steps to prevent exposure to habits and situations that will create or deepen addictions that lead to loss of self-control. A gambling addict does well in making sure that he never sets foot in a casino (perhaps by taking an exclusion order). It would be extremely difficult and foolish to try self-control inside a casino!

Fasting

Fasting is as ancient as the Bible. Jesus fasted in the desert and we have the temptation accounts in the context of fasting. Fasting helps us to master our appetites and discover our addictions.

There are many kinds of fasts. There is, of course, fasting from food, which is the commonest form of fasting. Jesus fasted for 40 days and nights, at the end of which He was tempted by Satan to satisfy His hunger through a miracle that was not within the will of the Father.

In his book *The Three Edwards,*[10] Thomas Costain described the life of two brothers:

> "Raynald III [was] a 14th-century duke in what is now Belgium. Grossly overweight, Raynald was commonly called by his Latin nickname, Crassus, which means fat.
>
> After a violent quarrel, Raynald's younger brother Edward led a successful revolt against him. Edward captured Raynald but did not kill him. Instead, he built a room around Raynald in the Nieuwkerk castle and promised him he could regain his title and property as soon as he was able to leave the room.
>
> This would not have been difficult for most people since the room had several windows and a door of near-normal size, and none was locked or barred. The problem was Raynald's size. To regain his freedom, he needed to lose weight. But

> Edward knew his older brother and each day he sent a variety of delicious foods. Instead of dieting his way out of prison, Raynald grew fatter.
>
> When Duke Edward was accused of cruelty, he had a ready answer: 'My brother is not a prisoner. He may leave when he so wills.'
>
> Raynald stayed in that room for 10 years and wasn't released until after Edward died in battle. By then his health was so ruined he died within a year — a prisoner of his own appetite."

There are many like Raynald, who are prisoners of their own appetite, whether it is lust, greed, gluttony or something else. Had Raynald fasted, he could have fasted his way out of his own prison and found true freedom. Alas, his appetite mastered him and he had no self-control.

There are other ways of fasting. One can fast from speaking, the need for applause, unnecessary activism, excessive shopping, emails, the computer and other modern gadgets, and many other things to which modern people are addicted. When we are able to fast from these things, we discover whether they master us or whether we have mastery over them.

In the early 20th century, a Japanese psychiatrist by the name of Shoma Morita (1874-1938) developed a therapeutic method called Morita Therapy.[11] The treatment begins with a week of isolated bed-rest. This week is of particular interest to us. The usual stimulation from reading, speaking, social interaction, writing, and so on would be withdrawn from the person who is isolated in a bare small room with nothing except a mattress. He is fed regularly with simple fare. The experience of such patients is as follows. Initially, they feel a physical restfulness being away from all social expectations and pressures.

A sense of gratitude follows as they remember the important people in their lives who had contributed significantly in their wellbeing and development. Then will come a restlessness and boredom when they begin to miss things and long for them — be it the newspapers or reading a book. It could be other things — applause and attention, the need to feel useful, shopping, and so on. What becomes clearer to them is an appreciation of their internal addictions. They begin to recognise the things that had come to master them.

Fasting does the same. It reveals our true inner condition, our weaknesses and addictions, and our sinful impulses. In this way, the spiritual habit of fasting may enable us to face ourselves in God's presence and help us in our pursuit of holiness in Christ and the freedom that comes from the power of the Holy Spirit.

Submission to Christ

Biblical self-control is not so much a stoic attempt to keep things in order within ourselves. Rather, it is allowing the rule of Christ to be experienced in our lives. Oswald Sanders explains that "(no) rapid growth in Christian maturity will be attained until the first indispensable step of submission to the lordship of Christ has been taken. The key question that determines whether or not He has been given that place of authority in the life is, 'Who makes the decision?'"[12]

When we submit to the lordship and rule of Christ, we experience self-control. This can be seen in key areas of our lives.

Christ Rules our Thoughts

We saw earlier how Paul calls for every thought to become obedient to Jesus Christ (2 Corinthians 10:5). Does this mean that we become robots and are not allowed to think our own thoughts? No, it does not mean that. Our thoughts are often ruled by our own sinful nature and they will go, in this case, into wrong and harmful directions. At times, our thoughts can also be hijacked and made use (or abused) by Satan.

The demon-possessed man in the area of Gerasenes is a case in point (Mark 5:1-20). Tormented by demons, his mind was a broken wasteland. He spent his days and nights where the tombs were, crying out and inflicting self-injury. The poor man was totally out of control, but his encounter with Jesus resulted in his deliverance. The demons having been cast out by Jesus, the man was sitting near Jesus, "dressed and in his right mind" (Mark 5:15). His mind was now under proper control and in a balanced state.

When Christ rules our mind, it means that like a benevolent ruler, He has freed us from forces that twist, torment and distort our thinking. We are then able to think thoughts that are congruent with who we are created to be. This, however, is not to be confused with mechanically regurgitating the thoughts of Christ. We will not function as automatons or puppets under God's control.

Paul advised the Corinthian Christians who were having chaotic worship services in the name of being under the influence of the Holy Spirit, that "God is not a God of disorder but of peace" and that "the spirits of prophets are subject to the control of prophets." Spirit-filled Christians would be in full control of their faculties. When we are under the control of the Spirit, we will be in control of ourselves. Biblical self-control is possible only in the presence of the rule of Christ.

Martin Luther wisely observed that "the idle mind is a devil's workshop." The problem with an undisciplined mind is that it can be taken over by the sinful flesh and the devil. They can work together to turn our thoughts towards dishonouring God and harm us. We may remember King David when he stayed back in Jerusalem when his army was at war (2 Samuel 11). In the idleness of his day, he lost control over his desires and his thinking (which turned into murderous directions and all kinds of denial and rationalisation). He fell grievously into sin.

Recall Peter's great confession about the identity of Jesus in Caesarea Philippi and how Jesus commended him by saying "Blessed are you, Simon son of Jonah" (Matthew 16:17). Yet, in the passage following, when Jesus revealed details about His death and resurrection, Peter rebuked Him with a "Never, Lord!" Peter had his own thoughts about the matter. But Jesus recognised the evil one who was behind Peter's thoughts at that moment. He rebuked Peter by saying, "Get behind me, Satan! You are a stumbling block to me; you do not have in mind the things of God, but the things of men" (Matthew 16:22-23). Jesus then made several statements about self-denial that are truths that must guide our lives, truths that will prevent our minds from going out of control.

On his part, Paul offers sound advice. He urges his readers to practise thinking godly thoughts: "Finally, brothers and sisters, whatever is true, whatever is noble, whatever is right, whatever is pure, whatever is lovely, whatever is admirable — if anything is excellent or praiseworthy — think about such things" (Philippians 4:8). Such focused and disciplined thinking (which would be aided by meditating on God's Word, reading good Christian books, including good biographies,[13] and singing the hymns of the church) is connected with the peace that "transcends all understanding" which "will guard your hearts and minds in Christ Jesus" (Philippians 4:7). Self-control includes the peaceful possession of one's mind.

Christ Rules our Emotions

The Lord also rules over our emotions. The guarding of the hearts and minds mentioned in Philippians 4:7 includes the emotions. In all situations we are called not to be anxious but to find the peace that is in Christ. Even in the emotional storms of our hearts, Christ can rule over us and still the storms. John Wesley, on his way to serve as a missionary in Georgia, America, was in a ship that was about to sink in a fierce storm. His heart was in turmoil as he feared impending death, but he was amazed (and further disturbed) when he witnessed the peaceful response of a group of Moravian believers who were also in the ship. Their emotions were calm as they sailed a raging sea and faced death. Only a few years later did Wesley find that peace and the Lord who rules over our anxious feelings. God used him to begin the Methodist movement.

Methodists were well-known for the way they died. With Christ ruling their hearts, they met their deaths with a deep calm and faith. Wesley himself died in that way.

Our emotions can go haywire. They can take us for a ride and a spiritual wild-goose chase. In the modern culture which encourages people to just follow their hearts, we must realise the dangers associated with such a faulty enterprise. As Christians, we are called to follow Jesus rather than our hearts. This means that all emotions we feel must be subject to the rule of Christ. High feelings can make us do foolish things; they can lead to pride, and can make people fall into sin. It is not unknown that after a spiritual high, there is a greater danger of sin and backsliding. This has been observed in revivals.

Low emotions must also be brought into subjection to Christ. They can take us down a path of doubt and disobedience, cynicism and depression. We have to bring all our emotions to Jesus and let Him rule us. Then we will have self-control over our emotions too.

Christ Rules our Will

Jesus, through the Spirit, will enable us to choose everything in a godly and God-pleasing way. We have the promise that God is at work in us, "to will and to act according to his good purpose" (Philippians 2:13). This takes place when we subject our will to the rule of Jesus and the power of the Holy Spirit. Then we will find a power within us that will make us do things that are in the path of righteousness. We will exercise self-control in the way we make choices, even as we walk along paths that are noisy with distractions and allurements.

We may remember the demoniac who was delivered by Jesus. He had full possession of his mind and will. He was no longer unable to control himself, but was "sitting there, dressed and in his right mind" (Mark 5:15). The man with restored control over his will was like a train driver who peacefully drove his train over the tracks.

We end by remembering that self-control is a fruit of the Holy Spirit. It arises when we surrender ourselves to Jesus our King and Master and are filled with the empowering and liberating Holy Spirit. Christ will truly rule over us in the various aspects of our lives. Then we will be able to exert self-control over our lives in all those same areas. In this sense self-control will come quite easily. It is not an uphill task that we try to achieve through self-effort — that will result in frustration and failure. But as the Spirit enables us, and as we cooperate with the Spirit in the exercise of spiritual habits and disciplines, then we will find that we have an easier time with self-control. When the King's rule is strong in the land, then the policeman's job is much easier.

The life that is marked by self-control will be a peaceful and beautiful one. It will bring glory to God, wholesomeness to the person, and blessings to others. It will have its own spiritual attraction as it reflects the rule of Christ in our lives and the restoration of order in our hearts, minds and souls.

Questions for Reflection

1. Discuss the example of Samson. In what ways does he represent the impulsive life? How does the modern world promote impulsive living and what evidence is there that people are losing control of themselves. How does this contrast with the Spirit-controlled life?

2. Discuss the difference between Stoicism and Christian self-control as shown in this chapter. What lessons can you learn for your own spiritual formation?

3. How did Jesus display self-control? Why is it important to submit to Him even as we live in a world of addictions and false masters? How can we practise daily submission to Him?

4. How can you practise fasting in its various forms? Why is it important? What are the benefits of Spirit-empowered self-control?

13

BEARING THE FRUIT OF THE SPIRIT

We have come a long way from where we began. We saw the Trinitarian roots of the fruit of the Spirit as listed by Paul in Galatians. We examined in detail each aspect of this fruit of the Spirit and saw how it reflected the character of Jesus and the many characteristics of His love. We also looked at the spiritual dynamics involved in the production of this spiritual fruit and the part that we are expected to play in cooperating with God's grace. We now end by looking at why the topic of our discussion is of such great importance.

The Importance of the Fruit of the Spirit

There are three reasons why the fruit of the Spirit, as listed by Paul, is critically important in the Christian life.

Firstly, the fruit of the Spirit has to do with God's eternal purposes for us. We noted at the beginning of this book that God's purpose for us is to make us like His Son Jesus Christ. When God created the first man and woman, they were made in the image of God. But sin, which has to do with the human rebellion against God, has terribly and tragically marred this image. In Christ, God is reconciling this estranged world to Himself (2 Corinthians 5:19), and re-establishing His rule which lies at the heart of the Kingdom of God. It is for this reason that Jesus began His ministry declaring that the Kingdom of God has come, inviting His listeners to repent and allow God's grace to touch their lives. Throughout His ministry, the focus in the teachings of Jesus was the Kingdom of God.

After Jesus rose from the dead, He spent 40 days with His disciples "speaking about the kingdom of God" (Acts 1:3). Paul, one of those touched by the Spirit of God, is depicted at the end of the book of Acts as being in prison in Rome for the sake of Christ, spending his time preaching the kingdom of God (Acts 28:31). It was this same Paul who wrote to the Romans about God's eternal purpose. Christians are "predestined [by God]...to be conformed to the likeness of his Son" (Romans 8:29-30).

The whole vocabulary of our salvation experience is built on the "alphabet" of God's unchanging and eternal purpose of restoring us to the likeness of His Son Jesus Christ. This central purpose is the basic building block of all that God is doing for and in us. This purpose lies at the heart of God's grand design to establish His rule in His universe. The rule of God will result in the character of Christ being reproduced in human beings, and the fruit of the Spirit deals with the character of Christ. God's eternal purpose is thus connected with the fruit of the Spirit — which has to do with the Kingdom of God.

Secondly, the fruit of the Spirit is the necessary evidence of God's work in us. The Christian experience is essentially an inner experience, because it is built on our encounter and relationship with the invisible God. God works in our hearts, souls and minds. This can neither be measured by scientific instruments, nor seen by our human eyes. They are hidden from our eyes, like what went on in the Holy of Holies in the ancient temple in Jerusalem or at the top of Mount Sinai and in the tent that Moses entered to commune with God (Exodus 33:7-11; 34:29-35). What went on within the shroud of mystery was evidenced by what could be seen — the face of Moses (over which he put on a veil) glowed with the radiance of God following encounters with God.

Paul took this up in his Corinthian correspondence when he compared the experience of Moses with the even greater experience of Christians who live in Christ. Moses had to put on a veil "to keep the Israelites from gazing at it while the radiance was fading away" (2 Corinthians 3:13), but for Christians filled with the Spirit of Christ, the transformation is measured in ever-increasing glory" (2 Corinthians 3:18). This transformation is "into his likeness" — referring to the likeness of Jesus. In the case of Moses, what went on at the top of the mountain or inside the tent of meeting (both of which were covered by clouds and therefore remained hidden from human eyes) was evidenced by the radiance of the face of Moses.

In the case of Spirit-filled Christians following Jesus, what goes on inside their minds, hearts and souls is evidenced by the fruit of the Spirit — the character of Jesus. The fruit of the Spirit makes visible the invisible work of God within us. It is both a necessary proof of God's invisible work, as well as an essential outcome of that work. The person who is full of the "acts of the sinful nature" and who is devoid of the fruit of the Holy Spirit "will not inherit the kingdom of God" (Galatians 5:19-20) because there is no evidence of God's work of grace in him. But if there is within a person the invisible work of God, then the fruit of the Spirit in his character and conduct will be the visible evidence of it.

Thirdly, the fruit of the Spirit brings us to the heart of all reality — the triune God. If the reader has not already noticed, the fruit of the Spirit has to do with the Father's eternal purposes, the Son's character and the Spirit's ministry within us. When we focus on the fruit of the Spirit, we are focusing on the united purpose and ministry of all the Persons in the Trinity. We are led into the heart of who God is and realise His purposes, character and power. To display the fruit of the Spirit is then to display the reality of God in our world. This brings us to the fourth reason for the importance of the fruit of the Holy Spirit.

Fourthly, the fruit of the Spirit has practical and missiological significance. People may be convinced by the words we speak, but they are more likely to be convinced by our lives, which they can see. Paul wrote to the Corinthians about being ambassadors of Christ and ministers of reconciliation. He declared, "we try to persuade men" and in the same verse mentions that "*[w]hat we are* is plain to God" and also to his readers (2 Corinthians 5:11, emphasis added). Persuading others with the gospel of Jesus has to do with the kind of people we are, not just the words we use. That is why it is important for us to affirm that anyone who is in Christ is a "new creation" (2 Corinthians 5:17). Not only does his vocabulary change but his very character and conduct is transformed. The evidence for this is the fruit of the Spirit.

God is now making "his appeal through us" because by His grace and in the Spirit we become "the righteousness of God" (2 Corinthians 5:20-21). The righteousness of God is found in Jesus who displayed it perfectly in His life. In Him we can now become displayers of that same righteousness when, by the sanctifying power of the Holy Spirit, we bear the very character of Christ. When that happens, it has immense missiological significance. The world will be convinced of the truthfulness and power of the Good News and be drawn to its promise. There is no other way we can hope to win the world for Christ.

Grace and Discipline

We have repeatedly seen that the fruit of the Spirit is the result of surrendering to the transforming grace and power of God. This is rooted in trusting God and obeying Him fully, and is achieved when our hearts are filled with the Spirit of Christ.

From the beginning to the end, the entire process is powered and enabled by the grace of God, as Paul argued in his epistle to the Galatians.

The operation of God's grace does not preclude the need for our cooperation with God's grace. Total reliance on God's grace and power does not negate the need for the exercise of spiritual discipline in our lives. God is at work in the depths of our being, but we must also work out our salvation (Philippians 2:13). We work because God works, and the two "workings" are not mutually exclusive. Our work of spiritual discipline, when built on God's gracious work in us, will bear true spiritual fruit. It is the Holy Spirit's fullness that enables us to bear that fruit, but this also involves cultivation of that fruit as we consciously and intentionally keep our eyes on Jesus [illegible] seek to follow Him and emulate Him.

The previous chapters emphasised the importance of God's operation in our lives and our cooperation with God. Grace and spiritual cultivation go together. Total reliance on the Spirit's enabling power goes together with the careful study of the character of God as shown in Jesus, and the resolve and commitment to become like Jesus. The infusion of the Holy Spirit and the intention of the will are both working together in bringing forth the character of Jesus in our lives. Total trust in God's purposes and power (in the form of surrender and submission) and diligent effort (in the form of obedience and the cultivation of spiritual disciplines) would result in the bearing of spiritual fruit.

Weeds and Artificial Fruit

We must note the parable of the weeds told by Jesus (Matthew 13:24-30) and how He later explained the parable (Matthew 13:36-43). The farmer sows good seed in his field. But at night, when everyone was asleep, the farmer's enemy sowed weeds among the wheat. When his servants brought the matter to the farmer's attention and asked whether he wanted them to pull out the weeds, the farmer told them to wait till it was harvest time when the weeds could be collected to be burned. Jesus was referring to the judgment that is coming when the wicked and the righteous will have entirely different ends.

In his book, *Wrestling with Christ*, Italian spiritual writer Luigi Santucci explores this parable of Christ and turns its implications inward. He locates the parable not only in the world which has both good and evil men but also our inner worlds where both good and evil often coexist.

> "Every evening I lie down like that field under the stars and I'm that tangle of different grasses...the good stalks and bad stalks get inextricably interwoven...When I perform

> [illegible] erous innocence, straightaway some selfish [illegible] up — in the impulse to help, a vain self- [illegible] e consoling caress, a hint of lechery; in my [illegible] f thanksgiving, some base superstition."[1]

When [illegible] d and the bad seed were planted in the same field, it must have been impossible to tell the difference between them. Even when the plants were sprouting in the earliest of stages, it would have been difficult to tell them apart, but the differences will be more obvious as the plants grow. John Anderson has helpfully written about the need to be mindful of weeds and artificial fruits when we think of the fruit of the Spirit.[2] Anderson explains:

> "The fruit of the Spirit does not initially take the form of outward deeds, or even habits of life. Perhaps it will be well to borrow a word from older theologies and speak of "habitudes"...The fruit of the Spirit is a cluster of seeds which grow and appear at their appointed time. It is only after the sun has shined, the rain has fallen, the weeds have been pulled that the fruit becomes evident and can then be recognised as such."[3]

In this process of trusting God, obeying Him and cultivating spiritual disciplines, we must be mindful of weeds and artificial fruits. While weeds may be obviously different from the real spiritual fruit, artificial fruit may take greater discernment to distinguish. They are the work of the devil (or the self colluding with the devil) that produces qualities that superficially resemble the fruit of the Spirit but when examined more deeply will show that they have nothing to do with the Spirit's enabling or the character of Jesus. They may appear religious and even commendable but they hide the flesh that is operating behind and beneath them.

Anderson provides a list that attempts to compare the fruit of the Spirit with its opposite weeds and the artificial fruits that may superficially resemble it.[4]

The Fruit of the Spirit	The Artificial Fruit	The Weed
Love	limited love	hatred
Joy	temporary joy	sorrow
Peace	numbness, carelessness	anxiety, strife
Patience	laziness, insensitivity	impatience
Kindness	manipulation by kindness	pride
Goodness	hypocrisy	evil
Faithfulness	half-heartedness	infidelity
Meekness [gentleness]	false modesty	self-seeking
Self-control	choosing lesser goods	lack of control

Anderson explains these differences in his more detailed discussion of each characteristic of the fruit of the Spirit. While we need not look at them here, we just need to know that what Anderson calls the weeds are obviously works of the flesh, similar to the list Paul writes of the works of the flesh (Galatians 5:19-21). These would be more readily obvious — like when the proverbial Martians (green little men) would turn up at a wedding party. The artificial fruits are much more subtle — like the green little men disguised as ordinary human beings. On initial contact, and to the untrained eye, the disguise would not be spotted.

For Christians eager to cultivate the fruit of the Spirit in their lives, they have to not only reject the more obvious works of the rebellious flesh, but also exercise vigilance against the more subtle forms of self-deception that produce counterfeit spiritual fruit. They have to discern between love that has an agenda and love that is selflessly sacrificial, between mere happiness (and a good mood) and true joy, between stoic responses and true biblical self-control. Like the artificial fruits that are used for decorations, they may resemble the real thing, but when you examine them closely, they exhibit the same sinful motives that produce, more overtly, the works of the flesh that are immediately repulsive to anyone who seeks to be godly.

This means that it is important to have the feedback and guidance of other Christians — those who are our peers who are godly and discerning, or those who are more mature and able to practise spiritual discernment. We must know and be convinced that it is the Spirit of God who alone will produce real spiritual fruit.

Relationship and Virtue

We must end with the important observation that the fruit of the Spirit has to do with our continuing relationship with Jesus Christ. It is not a matter of coming up with a list of virtues that we hope to cultivate and then trying our best to achieve them through our efforts. Rather, it has to do essentially with coming to know Jesus Christ as Saviour and Lord, and committing ourselves to Him. It involves looking at Him not only to be saved from the penalty of our sins but also to be freed from the power of sin and eventually from the presence of sin in our lives. It calls for keeping our eyes fixed on Jesus who is both Saviour and Example so that as we gaze at Him, we begin to look like Him.

We know that people begin to look like what they look at often. They become like the objects of their affection (and worship). Therefore, one can look like one's spouse, or pet, or one can become "money-faced" after looking much at money (so the wisdom of our cultural idiom says). If we keep looking at Jesus we will begin to look like Him. Our transformation into the likeness of Jesus depends on our relationship with Him and on our remaining in Him (2 Corinthians 3:18).

Becoming like Jesus depends on our opening our lives to the Spirit of Jesus so that He will dwell within us and, through His power, allow Jesus to live in and through us. Without this spiritual dimension and dynamic, any attempt on our part to become virtuous, no matter how disciplined our attempts are, is bound to fail miserably. However, with this dynamic constantly in place, our spiritual disciplines will be able to bring forth a rich harvest of spiritual fruit.

Deep relationships require commitment and effort, as we know from our various relationships. A person who loves his family member will take time to build the relationship — by communicating, spending time with the person, praying for the person, and seeking the good of the person and his wellbeing. Likewise, effort is required in maintaining and building our relationship with Jesus and being focused on Him. Such a focus will be evidenced by the rich presence of the fruit of the Spirit. In other words, the pursuit of the virtuous life is only meaningful if it is based on the pursuit of Christ.

True Christian virtue is the result of a rich relationship with Jesus Christ. As we draw closer to Jesus we will be able to observe Him more closely (through the Word and the Spirit), and we will find ourselves bearing the very character of Jesus in our motives, thoughts, words, actions and our relationships. We will know that the fruit is not the result of self-effort, but of divine grace as we cooperate with that enabling grace when we surrender to Christ and obey Him.

No one can hope to become virtuous (such virtue having to do with both act and motive, and with divine love) without relating closely with Christ. And no one can be close to Christ and not become a virtuous person. The relationship produces the virtue, for to know Christ is to become like Him. As we walk with Jesus, getting to know, love and serve Him, we will find ourselves becoming more and more like Him as we make progress in the journey with Jesus.

Questions for Reflection

1. Discuss why the fruit of the Spirit has special importance in the Christian life. Why is it the necessary evidence of God's work in us? What is its missiological significance?

2. What is the connection between grace and discipline? What problems arise when a proper biblical balance is lost and the connection is absent or distorted?

3. Discuss the danger of artificial fruit. Review the diagram in the chapter differentiating the fruit of the Spirit from the artificial fruit and "weeds." How useful do you find this?

4. "True Christian virtue is the result of a rich relationship with Jesus Christ." Discuss this statement and its implications for your spiritual formation and growth.

5. What are key lessons you have learned from this book? Share some key decisions you have made as a result.

ENDNOTES

Preface

1. Edward Farley, *Theologia: The Fragmentation and Unity of Theological Education* (Philadelphia: Fortress, 1983), chapter 1.

2. Philip D. Kenneson, *Life on the Vine: Cultivating the Fruit of the Spirit in Christian Community* (Downers Grove: InterVarsity Press, 1999), 11-12.

Chapter 1: The Father's Purpose

1. The next few paragraphs are taken from my article "A Medical Perspective on Salvation" in Chua Choon Lan, ed., *Carry the Spices: Singaporean Doctors in Medical Missions and Pastoral Ministry* (Singapore: Medical Missions Foundation, 2007), 208-213.

2. John Wesley, *Sermons on Several Occasions*, translated into modern English by James D. Holway, 2nd ed., (Ilkeston, Derbys: Moorley's, 1996), 159.

3. Philip D. Kenneson, *Life on the Vine.*

4. C. S. Lewis, *Mere Christianity* (London: Fontana Books, 1955), 170-171.

Chapter 2: The Character of Jesus

1. John Stott, *The Radical Disciple* (Nottingham: Inter-Varsity Press, 2010), 32.

2. Eugene H. Peterson, *The Jesus Way: A Conversation in Following Jesus* (London: Hodder and Stoughton, 2007), 7.

3. Bill Donahue, *In the Company of Jesus: Finding Unconventional Wisdom and Unexpected Hope* (Leicester, England: Inter-Varsity Press, 2006), 11.

4. Ibid., 10.

5. George A. Maloney, *Prayer of the Heart* (Notre Dame, IN.: Ave Maria Press, 1981), 114.

6. Robert M. Solomon, "Contextual Spirituality" in *Dictionary of Christian Spirituality*, Glen G. Scroggie, ed., (Grand Rapids: Zondervan, 2011), 205-210.

7. There is a need for more dialogue about such cultural differences among Christians to foster better understanding. Adequate discussions on these cultural differences are largely absent even in the best of books on hospitality. See Christine D. Pohl, *Making Room: Recovering Hospitality as a Christian Tradition* (Grand Rapids: William B. Eerdmans Publishing Company, 1999).

8. Philip D. Kenneson, *Life on the Vine.*

9. David F. Wells, *Above All Powers: Christ in a Postmodern World* (Grand Rapids: William B. Eerdmans Publishing Company, 2005), 49-52. See also David F. Wells, *Losing Our Virtue: Why the Church Must Recover Its Moral Vision* (Grand Rapids: William B. Eerdmans Publishing Company, 1998), 104-145 where these points are expanded.

10. David F. Wells, *Above All Powers*, 51.

11. Calvin Miller, *Into the Depths of God: Where Eyes See the Invisible, Ears Hear the Inaudible, and Minds Conceive the Inconceivable* (Minneapolis: Bethany, 2000), 148.

12. Calvin Miller, *Into the Depths of God*, 156.

Chapter 3: The Fruit of the Spirit

1. D. A. Carson, *A Call to Spiritual Reformation: Priorities from Paul and His Prayers* (Nottingham: Inter-Varsity Press, 1992), 134.

2. Martin Goldsmith, *Jesus and His Relationships* (Carlisle, Cumbria: Paternoster Press, 2000), 21.

3. William Law, *A Serious Call to a Devout and Holy Life* (Wilton, Conn.: Morehouse-Barlow, 1982), 58.

4. Francois Fenelon, *Fenelon's Spiritual Letters* (Augusta, Maine: Christian Books, 1982), 190-191.

5. Maxie Dunnam and Kimberly Dunnam Reisman, *The Workbook on Virtues and the Fruit of the Spirit* (Nashvillle: Upper Room Books, 1998), 8.

6. Maxie Dunnam and Kimberly Dunnam Reisman, op. cit.

7. See J. Oswald Sanders, *The Best That I Can Be* (Singapore: OMF Books, 1984), 64-69. Also, John White, *The Fight* (Downers Grove: InterVarsity Press, 1976), 190-194.

8. Dallas Willard, *The Divine Conspiracy: Rediscovering Our Hidden Life In God* (London: Fount, 1998), 341-408.

9. Philip D. Kenneson, *Life on the Vine*, 18-19.

Chapter 4: Love: The Chief Fruit of the Spirit

1. C. S. Lewis, *The Four Loves* (New York: Harcourt Brace, 1960). Lewis also deals with the human loves in his fictional work, *Till We Have Faces* (New York: Harcourt Brace, 1956).

2. Dennis Lennon, *Fuelling the Fire: Fresh Thinking on Prayer* (Bletchley, Manchester: Scripture Union, 2005), 21-22.

3. Jack O. Balswick and Judith K. Balswick, *The Family: A Christian Perspective on the Contemporary Home*, 3rd edn., (Grand Rapids: Baker Academic, 2007), 20-25.

4. Robert M. Solomon, *The Conscience: Rediscovering the Inner Compass* (Singapore: Armour Publishing, 2010), 202-216.

5. R. Somerset Ward, *To Jerusalem: Devotional Studies in Mystical Religion* (Harrisburg, PA.: Morehouse, 1994), 178.

Chapter 5: Joy: When Love Sings

1. *The Summa Theologica of St. Thomas Aquinas*, rev. ed., 1920; Online Edition by Kevin Knight, 2008, The first part of the second part, "Man's Last End" at http://www.newadvent.org/summa/2001.htm (accessed 13 February 2012). For another helpful work, see Brother Pierre-Yves, *Pleasure, Happiness, Joy*, Short Writings from Taize, no. 14 (Taize, France: Ateliers et Presses de Taizé, 2010).

2. Peter Kreeft, "Joy" at http://www.peterkreeft.com/topics/joy.htm (accessed on 13 February 2012).

3. Elton Trueblood, *The Humour of Christ* (San Francisco: Harper and Row, 1975).

4. John Pollock, *Wesley the Preacher: A Biography* (Eastbourne: Kingsway Publications, 1989), 98.

5. Charles Wesley, Where Shall My Wondering Soul Begin, *The United Methodist Hymnal*, (Nashville: United Methodist Publishing House, 1989), hymn 342.

6. J. I. Packer, *Rediscovering Holiness: Know the Fullness of Life with God* (Ventura, CA: Regal, 2009), 115-123.

7. *The Writings of John Bradford*, Vol. I, ed. Aubrey Townsend, (Cambridge: The University Press, 1848), 22-23.

Chapter 6: Peace: Love at Rest

1. Horatius Bonar, *God's Way of Holiness* (Chicago: Moody Colportage Library, n.d.), 3.

2. Gary Thomas, *The Beautiful Fight: Surrendering to the Transforming Presence of God Every Day of Your Life* (Grand Rapids: Zondervan, 2007), 209.

3. J. I. Packer, *Knowing God* (London: Hodder and Stoughton, 1973). See also J. I. Packer, *Knowing God: Study Guide* (Leicester: Inter-Varsity Press, 1993). A. W. Tozer, *The Knowledge of the Holy* (New York: HarperCollins, 1963).

4. Charles H. Spurgeon, *Devotions and Prayers of Charles H. Spurgeon*, ed. Donald Demaray (Grand Rapids: Baker Book House, 1960), quoted in *God's Treasury of Virtues* (Tulsa, OK,: Honor Books, 1995), 141-142.

5. Bernhard Erling, *A Reader's Guide to Dag Hammarskjöld's Waymarks* (St Peter, Minnesota: privately published, 2010), 178, available online at http://www.dhf.uu.se/wordpress/wp-content/uploads/2011/09/rg_to_waymarks.pdf

6. Berit Kjos, *A Wardrobe from the King*, (Wheaton, Ill.: Victor Books, 1988), 45-46.

Chapter 7: Patience: When Mature Love Waits

1. Kenneth S. Wuest, *Wuest's Word Studies: From the Greek New Testament*, vol. 1 (Grand Rapids: Wm. B. Eerdmans Publishing Company, 1973), 160.

2. See William D. Mounce, ed., *Mounce's Complete Expository Dictionary of Old and New Testament Words* (Grand Rapids: Zondervan, 2006), 501-502.

3. Stephen F. Wayward, *Fruit of the Spirit* (Leicester: Inter-Varsity Press; Grand Rapids: William B. Eerdmans Publishing Company, 1981), 120.

4. Charles Edward Jefferson, *The Character of Jesus* (New York: Thomas Y. Crowell Company, 1908), 277.

5. Jonathan Edwards, *Religious Affections*, (Edinburgh: Banner of Truth Trust, 1961), 277-279.

6. Charles Edward Jefferson, *The Character of Jesus*, 272-274.

7. Oswald Chambers, *Christian Disciplines* (Chennai, India: Evangelical Literature Service, 1999), 220.

8. John Duckworth, *Joan n the Whale and Other Stories You Never Heard in Sunday School* (Grand Rapids: Fleming H. Revell Co., 1987). This story is titled "The Man Who Built His House on the Rock."

9. See "The Three Races" by Darren Edwards at http://www.inspire21.com/stories/sportsstories/TheThreeRaces accessed on 1 March 2012.

10. Dietrich Bonhoeffer, *Life Together*, trans. John W. Doberstein (San Francisco, CA: Harper, 1954), 86.

11. See Henri Nouwen, *Adam: God's Beloved* (Marknoll: Orbis, 1997). See also Philip Yancey, "The Holy Inefficiency of Henri Nouwen," *Christianity Today*, 40:14, 9 December 1996, 80.

Chapter 8: Kindness: Love in Action

1. Ace Collins, *Stories Behind Women of Extraordinary Faith* (Grand Rapids: Zondervan, 2009), 190. This comment is attributed to Sophie Scholl, a German young lady who lived during the Nazi era and challenged its evils.

2. Robert Wuthnow, *Learning to Care: Elementary Kindness in an Age of Indifference* (New York: Oxford University Press, 1995).

3. Elisabeth Elliot, *A Lamp for My Feet: The Bible's Light for Your Daily Walk* (Ventura, CA.: Regal Books, 2004), 52-53.

4. A poem by Adelaide Proctor (1825-1864), quoted in L. B. Cowman, *Streams in the Desert*, ed. James Reimann (Grand Rapids: Zondervan, 1996), 229.

Chapter 9: Goodness: The Integrity of Love

1. Kenneth S. Wuest, *Wuest's Word Studies*, 160.

2. A. W. Tozer, *The Knowledge of the Holy* (India: Alliance Publications, 1961), 98-99.

3. Frank Wright, *Exploration into Goodness* (London: SCM Press, 1988), 84.

4. John Wesley in a letter to the Rev. Samuel Furley, March 30, 1754. *Letters of John Wesley*, ed. George Eayrs (London: Hodder and Stoughton, 1915), 423.

Chapter 10: Faithfulness: The Loyalty of Love

1. William D. Mounce, ed., *Mounce's Complete Expository Dictionary of Old and New Testament Words*, 234.

2. Katharine Doob Sakenfeld, *Faithfulness in Action: Loyalty in Biblical Perspective* (Philadelphia: Fortress Press, 1985), 135.

3. Katharine Doob Sakenfeld, *Faithfulness in Action*, p. 149.

4. Charles R. Swindoll, *The Quest for Character: Building a Faith to Withstand the Storms of Life* (Portland, Oregon: Multnomah Press, 1987), 195-196.

5. Art Beals, *Beyond Hunger*, quoted in Dwain Neilson Esmond, *24-7-365: One Year in the Word* (Hagerstown, MD.: Review and Herald Publishing Association, 2008), 186.

6. Eugene Peterson, *The Contemplative Pastor: Returning to the Art of Spiritual Direction* (Grand Rapids: William B. Eerdmans Publishing Company, 1989), 17.

7. Evelyn Underhill, *The Fruits of the Spirit* (Harrisburg, PA.: Morehouse Publishing, 1982), 28-29.

Chapter 11: Gentleness: The Beauty of Love

1. Stephen F. Winward, *Fruit of the Spirit*, 173.

2. Ibid.

3. C. Paul Willis, *Bells and Pomegranates: The Gifts and Fruit of the Spirit* (Shippensburg, PA.: Destiny Image Publishers, 1995), quoted in *God's Treasury of Virtues*, 362.

4. Henry Drummond, *The Greatest Thing in the World and 21 Other Addresses* (London: Collins, 1953), 130.

5. Jerry Bridges, *The Practice of Godliness* (Colorado Springs: NavPress, 1983), 221.

6. Adrian van Kaam, *Spirituality and the Gentle Life* (Denville, NJ,: Dimension Books, 1974), 37.

7. Iris Murdoch, *The Sovereignty of Good* (London: Routledge and Kegan Paul, 1970), 103-104.

8. Ibid., 59.

9. Judith C. Lechman, *The Spirituality of Gentleness: Growing Toward Christian Wholeness* (San Francisco: Harper and Row, 1989), 172.

Chapter 12: Self Control: When Love Submits to God

1. Kenneth S. Wuest, *Wuest's Word Studies*, 160.

2. Charles R. Swindoll, *Come Before Winter...And Share My Hope* (Portland, OR.: Multnomah Press, 1985), 211.

3. Everett Ferguson, *Backgrounds of Early Christianity* (Grand Rapids: William B. Eerdmans Publishing Company, 1987) , 294.

4. Eugene H. Peterson, *The Jesus Way*, 31.

5. Ibid.

6. Fifth Rule in "Rules for the Discernment of Spirits" in *The Spiritual Exercises of St. Ignatius Loyola*, trans. Elder Mullan, (New York, P.J. Kennedy & Sons, 1914), found in http://www.sacred-texts.com/chr/seil/seil79.htm accessed on 20 February 2012.

7. Eugene H. Peterson, *The Jesus Way*, 35.

8. Charles R. Swindoll, *Come Before Winter*, 211.

9. See Gerald May, *Love and Grace: Love and Spirituality in the Healing of Addictions* (New York: HarperCollins, 1988), 42-90.

10. Thomas B Costain, *The Three Edwards* (Garden City, New York: Doubleday, 1962); the story is described by Rick Ezell, *The Seven Sins of Highly Defective People* (Kregel, 2003), 129-130.

11. David K. Reynolds, *The Quiet Therapies: Japanese Pathways to Personal Growth* (Honolulu: The University Press of Hawaii, 1980), 4-45.

12. Oswald Sanders, *Spiritual Discipleship: Principles of Following Christ for Every Believer* (Chicago: Moody Publishers, 1994), 82.

13. See Philip D. Kenneson, *Life on the Vine*, 171. He points out the importance of Christian biographies and "imitating the saints" in addition to reading the Bible.

Chapter 13: Bearing the Fruit of the Spirit

1. Luigi Santucci, *Wrestling with Christ* (London: Fontana Books, 1974), 117.

2. John W. Anderson, *The Fruit of the Spirit* (Phillipsburg: NJ: Presbyterian and Reformed Publishing Company, 1985), 36-44.

3. John W. Anderson, *The Fruit of the Spirit*, 41.

4. Ibid., 43.

INDEX

F

G

H

N

O

P

R

S

T

V

W

Popular Titles by Robert M Solomon

The Conscience

Though the conscience is a universal reality, it is increasingly forgotten in discussions, even in church. *The Conscience* enlightens the reader on the nature and functions of the conscience. It comprehensively examines what the Bible actually teaches about the conscience and what roles it plays in the experience of salvation and spiritual formation. Discover how the church can minister to the conscience through teaching, modelling and healing as Bishop Robert Solomon analyses the role of the conscience in key areas of our lives: the family, workplace, and the public square.

ISBN 13 : 978-981-4305-05-1
ISBN 10 : 981-4305-05-7
Book size : 229 by 152mm
No. of Pages : 264

The Prayer of Jesus

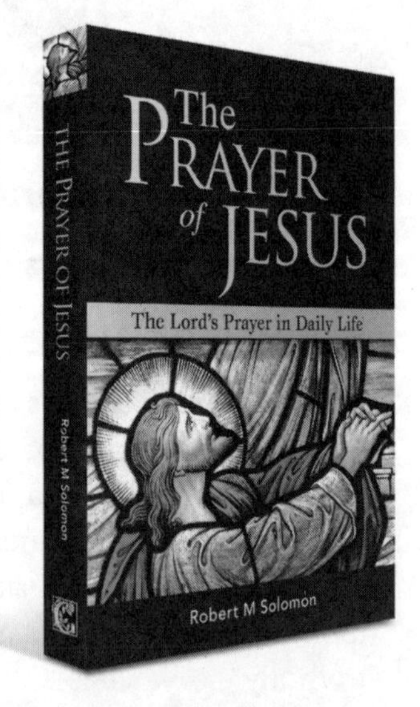

The Prayer that Jesus taught His disciples has had a significant role in the worship, thought and life of the historical church. This book draws from the rich history of this Prayer and explores its depths by examining each petition and clause in the Prayer in the illuminating light of biblical teaching and the perspective of the mind of Christ. The purpose is not only to foster deeper understanding but also to encourage a deeper allegiance to Jesus and a close union with Him in prayer, service and witness.

ISBN 13 : 978-981-4270-10-6
ISBN 10 : 981-4270-10-5
Book size : 229 by 152mm
No. of Pages : 312